BRAND AVATAR

BRAND AVATAR

TRANSLATING VIRTUAL WORLD BRANDING INTO REAL WORLD SUCCESS

Alycia de Mesa

First published 2009 by
PALGRAVE MACMILLAN

Palgrave Macmillan in the UK is an imprint of Macmillan Publishers Limited, registered in England, company number 785998, of Houndmills, Basingstoke, Hampshire RG21 6XS.

Palgrave Macmillan in the US is a division of St Martin's Press LLC, 175 Fifth Avenue, New York, NY 10010.

Palgrave Macmillan is the global academic imprint of the above companies and has companies and representatives throughout the world.

Palgrave® and Macmillan® are registered trademarks in the United States, the United Kingdom, Europe and other countries

ISBN-13: 978–0–230–20179–8
ISBN-10: 0–230–20179–2

This book is printed on paper suitable for recycling and made from fully managed and sustained forest sources. Logging, pulping and manufacturing processes are expected to conform to the environmental regulations of the country of origin.

A catalogue record for this book is available from the British Library.

A catalog record for this book is available from the Library of Congress.

10 9 8 7 6 5 4 3 2 1
18 17 16 15 14 13 12 11 10 09

Printed and bound in Great Britain by
CPI Antony Rowe, Chippenham and Eastbourne

This book is dedicated to brands, branders, tech geeks and the people who love them all.

CONTENTS

CONTENTS

LIST OF ILLUSTRATIONS

ACKNOWLEDGMENTS

This book could not have been completed without the assistance of some great people in the industry – especially Aliza Sherman, Steven Groves, Ann-Marie Mathis, Betsy Book and the many, many bloggers and social networkers who love to rant about virtual things. Thanks and love to my husband Bruce for putting up with crazy, late night schedules and to my children Kian and Kai for letting me sleep in the next day. Thanks also to Jo Lou Young for her positive support and graciously hearing my rants by phone. Many additional thanks to Alexandra Dawe, my lovely and recently new mommy editor, and the rest of the team at Palgrave Macmillan for supporting *Brand Avatar*.

ALYCIA DE MESA

INTRODUCTION

I remember as a ten-year-old kid being so excited about my new prize possession. Gifted to me by my uncle, I was the proud new owner of a matte white, Commodore Vic 20 personal computer. The year was 1981. As I recall, I barely knew what to do with it and had no idea what it was actually capable of, but I was determined to use it even if it meant playing Space Invaders until I could dream of nothing but Blue Meanies (and I think I did). Thus began my love affair with technology. It's true that life may have been more or less the same 20 years ago, but it's hard to believe that we didn't have laptop computers, faxes were still a luxury, and iPods and cell phones weren't even imagined:

> **"Those of us who take Second Life seriously like to compare it to the Web in 1994. The Web back then was slow, and a lot of the technologies we take for granted today hadn't been invented yet. Indeed, many smart people believed in 1994 that nobody would ever trust the Internet for e-commerce." —*Mitch Wagner***

As a branding and naming consultant in the 1990s, I was able to marry my branding skills with burgeoning new technologies known as dotcoms in San Francisco. It really was an exciting time to live in the Bay Area, because change, we all knew, was imminent. It was thick and palpable even if they didn't know it yet in Indiana. Everyday citizens were going to be interacting with technology in a way that would shape their everyday habits in a completely different way than they had known before. Groceries on demand delivered in vans, a vast array of books for purchase mailed straight to you, news and political information reaching every end of the Earth instantaneously, a new type of letter writing, which would trump all previous forms of communication, would become a daily routine and habit. And what was more new generations would grow up not knowing a world without this technological way of life.

I remember that when the Internet began to emerge for the masses, agencies, marketers and big brands alike just scratched their heads wondering what to do with this technological wonderland – much less how to explain what to do with it in regard to branding and marketing. It's funny to recall how marketing strategies involving coupons emailed to a consumer was a truly revolutionary idea in its day. E-commerce was a concept sneered at and highly distrusted, while designers were still trying to figure out the basics of web design. I even recall being red in the face, laughing hysterically the first time my best friend showed me what AOL chat room cybersex was like.

While everyone is well aware of the dotcom collapse at the end of the decade, what most people don't realize was during the time prior to the bubble bursting, there were a handful of innovative thinkers who were not only dreaming but actually creating three-dimensional (3D) virtual reality environments to be the next generation of the Internet. Some of them even convinced a few major brands to jump in on the great experiment, but more on that later.

As the new millennium has unfolded, a new wave of the Internet has presented itself with more in-depth ways to do the things that come most naturally to human beings: communicate, interact, and socialize with other people and to express individual creativity. Because the success of social media sites like Facebook, MySpace, YouTube, Twitter, etc. has led to increased interest in richer, more creative and collaborative forms of community, virtual worlds have and are filling a niche through not only their customization and personalization features, but through their highly visual and audio experience on the Internet – as if you had actually stepped into them. Inspired by video games and science fiction, virtual worlds are the much more graphic representation of social media on the Internet. Not so surprisingly, brands of various sorts are diving into these new interactive worlds hoping to capture tech-forward audiences with non-traditional marketing. The result is a chameleon of computers, entertainment and brand building that (hopefully) deliver a range of experiences versus one-way, marketing-driven messages.

Intel, the company, has stated that the digital universe itself is expanding. In 1998, Internet use was estimated to be 150 million users. As of 2008, that number is approaching a billion. Think Web 2.0 is just a silly catch phrase that will fade away? Think again. Although the present forms of virtual worlds such as with the big players: Second Life, There.com and Kaneva may ultimately not be the face of the 3D Internet, they are the great labs of experimentation necessary to get us there.

What this book is about is how the matrix of virtual worlds, business and brands come together. *Brand Avatar – Translating Virtual-World Branding into Real-World Success* is a look at business and branding strategies within the Internet's current landscape of virtual worlds. Virtual-world websites such as Second Life and There.com have already garnered millions of users around the world, representing a cross-section of ages, ethnicities and purchasing power. Virtual-world "residents" use and spend real money within the fictional-turned-real-life economies. Companies as diverse as Adidas, Saturn, Jean-Paul Gaultier, MTV, governmental agencies, and virtual-world agencies based on real-life marketing/media agencies have all plunged into these previously unchartered waters to give their brands a virtual presence, using an assortment of strategies and tactics:

> "While more traditional 'advertising-type' tactics can deliver a message, they don't provide an experience." —*Carol Kruse, vice president of Global Interactive Marketing at Coca-Cola*

Brand Avatar – Translating Virtual-World Branding into Real-World Success covers the emergence of virtual worlds, the culture and psychographic profile of virtual-world users, the companies represented and the effectiveness of their business and branding strategies as well as the challenges that have emerged as a result of these worlds such as creating worldwide virtual-world standards and intellectual property theft. The intent of the book is to provide an overview of the represented companies and then spotlight global brands such as Pepsi, CosmoGirl!, Playboy and others as specific case studies in strategy, creative execution and outcomes/effectiveness of their virtual campaigns and products. The book also covers "grass-root" brands found only on Second Life and reviews what lessons can be learned from their successes:

> "It's been said that there's too much brand noise out there to make much of a dent in the consumer's consciousness. So if this world's saturated, why not move on to the next virtual one?" —*Alycia de Mesa, brandchannel.com article 2007*

What this book is not about is in-world gaming otherwise known as MMPORGs (massively multiplayer online role-playing games) where many players come on-line and into 3D worlds to accomplish goal-oriented quests and tasks, such as the wildly

popular World of Warcraft. While a few MMOs that also incorporate virtual-world qualities are mentioned, the primary
focus is on virtual worlds that have communities combined
with in-world economies (featuring currencies and microtransactions).

Since beginning this project, one thing is very clear: change
is rampant and occurs with whiplash quickness when it comes
to virtual worlds. In 2006 and 2007, the press itself could find
almost nothing wrong with vws (virtual worlds) and hailed
them as the next great boom. By the end of the year, vws and
the brands within could seem to do nothing right. Old news is
a few seconds ago, but it's my hope that this book will take you
on a guided journey through the vw landscape, trends, and the
brands that are exploring these new worlds to create value for
everyone (and also happen to be learning many lessons along
the way). I hope you enjoy the show.

Sources

Coca Cola, available from: http://www.worldsinmotion.biz/2007/12/
cocacola_migrates_coke_studios.php

"Intel Silicon Innovation: Fueling New Solutions for the Digital Planet,"
available from: http://www.intel.com/technology/mooreslaw/index.
htm

Mitch Wagner, available from: http://www.informationweek.com/blog/
main/ archives/2007/09/the_future_of_v_1.html

1

THE EMERGENCE AND CHARACTERISTICS
OF VIRTUAL WORLDS

brand |brand|
noun
1 a type of product manufactured by a particular company under a particular name

avatar |ˈavəˌtär|
noun
1 an incarnation, embodiment, or manifestation of a person or idea

• derived from the Sanskrit word for the visible form that gods take on earth

"In a few years, I think everybody will walk around cyberspace as an avatar." —Franz Buchenberger, former President, Black Sun Interactive, as quoted in 1996

The programmer looks down at his hands and scans his arms and torso . . . they've been rendered. In a split second he realizes that his entire body is morphed into a seamless integration with the computer animated screen. He's not just playing the game, he's a *part* of the game. And what's more he can control the outcome of it, shaping his own world, his own experience and own destiny.

THE EARLY WORLDS

The year may have been 1982, but the scene from the Disney science fiction film *Tron* portrayed a graphic picture of life in the new millennium beginning to imitate art. Back then, Steve Lisenberger, *Tron*'s producer was, according to a Wikipedia entry, "frustrated by the clique-ish nature of computers and video games and wanted to create a film that would open this world up to everyone." Little did Steve know that only 20 years later his film would be echoed in the wave of the interactive and democratically collaborative Internet known collectively as "Web 2.0." or more colloquially as "social media". I've always found it interesting how science fiction entertainment tends to spark the imagination and inspire the genius of man to make something a reality – or on the flip side scare them enough to think twice about bringing something with potentially devastating effects to fruition.

A decade after *Tron* Neal Stephenson envisioned what he called a "metaverse" in his 1992 novel *Snow Crash*. The metaverse, a black ball 1.6 times the size of earth with a huge street around its equator, was what Stephenson called his virtual world where the novel's characters uploaded self-designed avatars to interact in the singular metaverse as they played, conducted business, went shopping, danced at nightclubs and strolled the streets while meeting and conversing with other virtual citizens. It held the vision for a 3D experience of surfing the Internet – and not long after, real-life companies from the corridors of Silicon Valley and Europe began to bring this fictional account to life.

Ever since the Industrial Revolution, man has been fascinated with technology dreamt by innovators such as da Vinci and others. The mad relationship of creating, using, and controlling technology to do bigger and better things – to make man more productive, more powerful and somehow larger

8

than life is what spurs us to keep creating and engaging with technology. And yet, the awesome force of technology's power makes us feel the exhilarating rush of riding its super-human abilities *and* absolutely fear the control it may have over us.

There are many gruesome sci fi tales of technology gone awry to lament over and point at due to the dark nature of man. A simple recall of Orwell's *1984*, *Bladerunner*, the retina-reading billboards that adjust an ad based on the profile of the passerby in *Minority Report*, and many other similarly themed films and literature are testament that more than anything, we fear the loss of our freedom and selves to the bidding of ever-more sophisticated technology. But lest we digress, that is not the point of this book.

You need only to look to technology's trends – both hardware and software – to see what percentage of the population dives head first into the bleeding-edge of new technology, and what percentage stands back, saying "now wait a minute . . . I think I need to wait and see about this" – or how many even get angry that they may have to deal with change *yet again*. And there are how many more that dig their boots into the sand and resist changing at all.

Technology is all about change. And as such, some people embrace the thrill of its unknown, chaotic nature, and others pull an ostrich moment and put their heads in the proverbial sand out of sheer fear. Whenever a new technology trend comes along, there are obvious cycles and patterns of adoption. What I'm about to go over has been cited in a host of ways and variations on a theme in various business and innovation books. While the concepts presented below are not new, it's important to re-state them to put virtual worlds into context to other trends.

In the beginning there are those pioneers who begin using a technology just after the developers release them. Maybe the pioneers are friends, colleagues, or social media buddies of the developers or avid followers of developer message boards. They are the people who love tech to the nth degree and are hungry to try something new to either bash it to bits or extol its virtues to anyone who can tolerate the unabashed tech accolades. Everything is about the now and the new – brownie points if there are vestiges of tech hall of fame past in the mix. This is what is often referred to as the *"bleeding edge of technology."*

Once a technology gets past the intense scrutiny of pioneers, it begins to fall into the hands of the influencers. These are likely to be the pioneer's slightly less nerdy friends, colleagues, social media types, bloggers or other tech trend followers on the constant prowl for something new. This is the early adoption, *"leading edge of technology"* pointing innovatively (and hopefully positively) toward a better future. Perhaps this is a purely subjective viewpoint, but in my own observations, the influencers, while still early adopters, seem to *want* to find something to champion and are ever so slightly less critical of a technology versus the intense scrutiny of pioneers.

Most start-up technologies fall off at or between the bleeding and leading edges. To push beyond the pioneering stages takes the acceptance of those who were not necessarily first on board the technology train but are early enough to influence others into considering the technology's appeal. The success of the influencers is coupled with the rage of the media machine, which, with the necessary critical mass, gets the technology into the hands of the mainstream user.

What's interesting about the media is that as we look at this first decade of the new millennium, never has the media been so fragmented and specialized – and the blur between traditional media and social media is only growing. A technology has never had so many ways to capture the attention of the media to bring it into critical mass: RSS feeds; micro-blogging sites (such as Twitter) to break news articles; bookmarking sites (such as Digg and del.icio.us) to share articles; individual and traditional media outlet bloggers (such as the Huffington Post or Howard Kurtz for the Washington Post); web-based articles that come before a radio, TV or print story breaks; and Internet articles that appear and are archived after a story breaks through the traditional media channels. The hope, of course, is that the technology will ride the massive wave propelled by the influencers and media to tip over into the accepting hands of the mainstream. How long and how wide that gulf between influencers and mainstream is, is what puts many a company and venture capitalist on edge.

THE ADOPTION CONTINUUM

There is talk all over the Internet, media, and tech and marketing folks alike about this new wave of the Internet (usually dubbed Web 2.0 by the press and by users, social media) that has been brewing – something akin to and as big (if not bigger) than the happenings of the early- to mid-1990s original wave of dotcoms. *But what in Web 2.0 are virtual worlds exactly?* Virtual worlds are generally accepted as being computer-based simulated environments where users of the worlds are represented by avatars, which are visually depicted by textual, two-dimensional (2D) or 3D graphics. Virtual worlds provide environments ranging from fantasy (such as Gaia), themed (such as Disney), to create-your-own-reality modeled world (such as There.com: see screenshot 1A and Second Life: see Screenshot 1B). Although not all virtual worlds allow for more

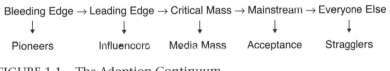

FIGURE 1.1   The Adoption Continuum

SCREENSHOT 1A/1B   Cybertown Prototype

than one avatar to interact with one another, the worlds that have garnered the most attention by the media and marketers are those that allow a multi-user, real-time experience. Wikipedia expands on the definition of virtual worlds by stating: "The model world may simulate rules based on the real world or some hybrid fantasy world. Example rules are gravity, topography, locomotion, [and] *real-time actions and communication*. Communication between users is varied from text and graphical icons to visual gesture, sound, and rarely, forms using touch and balance senses." It's worthy to note that even the definition above is changing rapidly. To illustrate just how quickly technology evolves within these worlds, from the time it took to begin and end this book, communication between avatars in Second Life has evolved from text chat via typing on a keyboard to real-time voice chat options through VoIP (Voice Over Internet Protocol) and since editing this book, it now offers Instant Messaging – and that's very old news.

Most people don't realize that the evolution of virtual worlds goes all the way back to the late 1960s with the emergence and use of the first virtual-reality simulators for military training purposes and the development of ARPANET by the US Department of Defense which would eventually become what we now know as the Internet. In 1978, the first multi-user, online game called "MUD" (Multi-User Dungeon) was developed and is credited as the "world's oldest virtual world" (www.british-legends.com). A text-based game played by using a TELNET program, players could congregate together to engage one another in a fantasy-based environment with the object of becoming a witch or wizard and, of course, getting the most points. (Believe it or not, it can still be played online today in the original format at: http://www.british-legends.com.)

The idea of more than one person playing a game together, regardless of where they are in the world, has always been a popular one with technocrats. What MUD started eventually became the realm of MMORPG (massively multi-player online role-playing game) the first one of which (with a graphical interface) was "Habitat" launched by LucasFilm for the Commodore 64 personal computer in 1985. Today more than hundreds of MMORPGs exist including World of Warcraft and Star Wars Galaxies which attract teens to middle-aged accountants alike.

By the time Neil Stephenson's Snow Crash emerged in 1992 as a glimpse-of-the-future sci fi novel, the modern Internet was just emerging into the public domain and a working prototype of virtual worlds as a 3D interface to web sites and especially e-commerce shop-fronts, called "Cybertown," was designed and developed by Philippe Van Nedervelde (who would shortly thereafter found E-SPACES, which produces virtual worlds to this day). It was the first PC-based 3D virtual world prototype to incorporate aspects of what we now think of as a 3D virtual world. The prototype was commissioned by the strategy department of Swedish telecom giant Ericsson – Business Networks Division (now Sony Ericsson).

As Van Nedervelde tells it:

"The prototype showed a town square, featuring trees and a fountain, with around it a collection of shops, services

and Ericsson's own office building. Over half of these
could be entered: an art shop with some 3D artifacts – like
a glass vase and a textured wooden bowl – on display with
which the user could interact (and examine the sticker –
some of which were shocking indeed); a bank featuring a
working mock-up of an indoor ATM and a travel agency
featuring a 3D globe of the Earth through which users
could interactively specify and book their trips."

Ericsson's office building featured a reception, a water cooler,
two furnished meeting rooms and an office supplies & productivity software shop for employees that featured interactively manipulable boxes of the software as well as of the office
supplies. A dialog system embedded in the 3-D world showed
the price of these items and demonstrated how employees
might order them. . . The goal was to confront them with one
of the shapes of the future of telecommunications."

According to Van Nedervelde, Ericsson successfully used
the prototype internally as intended to broaden the minds of
its key decision makers and executives. E-SPACES, the company which Philippe Van Nedervelde founded after the
Cybertown prototype, went on to produce interactive 3-D virtual environments which mimicked real-life environments
and scenarios for real world applications such as maritime
and airport training simulation and online banking for
Russian, Spanish and eventually U.S. clients over the next few
years. These original city and village depicting graphical interfaces served as the inspiration for much of what is actually
used today.

By the fall of 1995, E-SPACES embarked on its first experiment with a working 3-D virtual world system called "Milena."
One of the very first Internet-based 3D chat environments, it
enabled users to text chat with one another in real time while
exploring a three-dimensional space representing the Madrid

SCREENSHOT 1C   Second Life

nightlife. Milena included an alternative version reported to have been created for the electronic art festival in Spain Art Futura '95 where visitors could explore a virtual art gallery of Spanish art and leave comments and messages about the art.

Van Nedervelde contends that Milena was "neither complete nor robust" but rather developed to identify issues of "constructing cyberspace on the Internet." Tandem Computers Inc. out of Cupertino, California, who were the original joint venture co-founders of and investors in E-SPACES, bought the Milena source code and made the client, server and source code available online to "encourage debate and development of on-line worlds."

In San Francisco, a company called Worlds Inc. introduced an Internet virtual environment called "Alpha World," where avatars chatted with other avatars in a 3D environment. As the company built 3D virtual worlds for corporate clients such as IBM, Visa, and Coca-Cola, Worlds also found other

SCREENSHOT 1D   There.com

ways to experiment with vws including a partnership in a project that gave seriously ill children new opportunities to play in a virtual world using avatars.

The only problem was Worlds as a company had just launched, and it was the mid 1990s – the same time the Internet dotcoms were riding the massive wave over to mainstream users and at a time when broadband Internet access connections were rare. Despite World's handful of multinational large corporations on-board with virtual world experiments for marketing purposes, the medium couldn't take off fully due to the bandwidth limitations. Gen Suzuki, then managing director of NTT's Interspace project and client of Worlds, so believed in the power of the 3D net that he told the New York Times "avatars would become a necessary part of a vast network that focuses on communication between people rather than between people and information, as today's Internet does." The year was 1996.

During this same period Black Sun Interactive, a tech company based in Munich, Germany specializing in 3D environments, was also looking to bring virtual worlds to the web with its Cybergate and Cyberhub programs. In the same New York Times article, Franz Buchenberger, then president of Black Sun, "shrugged off the skepticism surrounding avatars, and insisted that all technical barriers to their acceptance would disappear within two or three years."

THE ESTABLISHERS

Despite development of other worlds in the 1990s and early 2000s such as VZones, There.com, Worlds.com, Muse, TowerChat, whyrobbierocks.com, and Second Life (the latter of which heavily incorporated many of the graphical aspects described earlier), it wasn't until 2006 and 2007 that the media machine started to pick-up on the unique, sci fi and rather sensationalistic aspects of virtual worlds such as Second Life and There.com in large part because money exchanged hands in a free market economy and real-life wealth was being created as a result. Suddenly these descendants of *Snow Crash* like There.com, Second Life and Cyworld emerged as not only a place to create and hang out as an altar ego avatar, but a place to do good old-fashioned commerce as well. And where there are people and commerce, there are brands.

Sources

E-spaces First Cybertown Prototype, available from: http://www.e-spaces. com/lbw/portfolio/projects/port_cybertown.htm
E-spaces Milena, available from: http://www.e-spaces.com/lbw/portfolio/ projects/port_milena.htm

New York Times, available from: http://query.nytimes.com/gst/fullpage.
html?res=9A0DE4D81E39F937A35750C0A960958260&sec=&spon=
&pagewanted=2
Stephenson, N. (1992) *Snow Crash*, Harmondsworth: Penguin.
Lisenberger, S. (1982) *Tron*, available from: http://209.85.173.104/
search?q=cache:6DK9ARh-ItkJ:en.wikipedia.org/wiki/Tron_(film)+
tron&hl=en&ct= clnk&cd=3&gl=us&client=firefox-a
Virtual World History, available from: http://www.avatarplanet.com/
history.php
Virtual World Review, available from: http://www.virtualworldsreview.
com/cybertown/
Wikipedia, available from: http://en.wikipedia.org/wiki/Virtual_world

2

THE CULTURE OF VIRTUAL WORLD USERS

"Virtual world users speak a different language and have a different culture – indeed, virtual worlds are made up of so many cultures of the mind that the majority of the world, which does not yet use them, can only make it more confusing to generalize when they do come into these worlds." —*Taran, Blogger*

Contrary to popular belief, virtual world users may be on the forward edge of technology, but they're not all geeky pubescent teens and college students who may see the light of day once a week. Users represent a cross-spectrum of society based on age, profession, marital/familial status, income, etc., and contrary to stereotypes, many *are* inherently social by nature and truly believe in the power of social media connecting people together in a way that improves the quality of life.

I remember in 2007 being interviewed for a Brazilian business magazine called *Amanha* shortly after I wrote an article for Brandchannel about virtual-world branding. The question (which I paraphrase) came up: "Are people going to use virtual worlds to replace meeting people in real life?" At first I laughed that a professional interviewer would ask such a funny and almost paranoid question. Then I realized her question was what is on most people's minds: are we going to a place with technology where real life doesn't matter much?

My answer then and still is an emphatic "no." If that were the case, then chat rooms a la AOL from the 1990s would have already rendered societies anti-social. If anything there is evidence that virtual-world behavior and experiences actually have an impact on behaviors in real life. There is much talk in the public domain that virtual-world users are in-world to live out an altar ego far removed from their every day life one – in other words virtual worlds become a means for fantasy role-playing and sometimes to an extreme. Mary Ellen Gordon of Market Truths recently conducted extensive market research in Second Life regarding psychographics. What she found was that by and large behavior corresponds more to real life than some sort of fantasy life played out in-world. "Prior to beginning research in SL, I had read a lot of speculation about people using avatars to enact some sort of fantasy life, and I still hear and read that sort of conjecture fairly frequently (though typically not from people who spend a lot of time in virtual worlds themselves). This is an issue we've looked at in a number of different contexts, and what we've found is that some people may use avatars to enact fantasies some of the time, but that does not apply to most people most of the time in SL. Role-playing may be more common in other virtual worlds, but at least in SL there is a fairly close correspondence (in attitudes and behaviors – not necessarily physical appearance) between the majority of RL people and their avatars."

ADULT USER PROFILES AND HABITS

In a fairly non-descript room in the middle of Stanford University's campus, sit assistant professor of communication Jeremy Bailenson and his "Virtual Human Interaction Lab" where he and a handful of graduate and undergraduate students explore human behavior in virtually-based realities and its effects after coming out of the virtual reality into real life. Bailenson and his companion researchers are putting the science into virtual realities, meticulously recording the outcomes of various experiments within computer-generated virtual worlds – a field that is just beginning to take off. (Jaron Lanier, the visionary who coined the term "virtual reality" and founded the first company to sell virtual reality equipment back in the days of wires, large suits and even larger gloves has said that back in the 1980s, "We had the gloves and bodysuits – we couldn't help but try these things anecdotally, but that's not science, that's *storytelling.*")

According to an article written in January 2008 Stanford's Business Alumni, "Studies in Bailenson's lab are showing that experience gained via digital alter egos can change how people behave in real life – at least in the short term." From virtual exercising, to studies on financial decisions, to stepping into an aged version of you or even a KKK (Ku Klux Klan) outfit, studies are being conducted around Stanford's hallowed halls to see the effects of different behaviorally-based scenarios within virtual realities, and what the immediate outcomes are (if any) on real-life behaviors. While not all studies are conclusive in their findings, the overall theme seems to indicate that there is a difference noted in real-life behaviors even if it's very short term.

Virtual realities are indeed a funny paradox and intersection of fantasy, entertainment and altar egos. While some users may choose to create an avatar who looks and behaves 180 degrees opposite of their everyday person/personality, many more are within a lesser degree of their actual persona with a bit of an uninhibited boost from the anonymity factor of their online presence.

Whether you take the true gaming worlds such as War of the Worlds or Star Wars Galaxies or reality-based social worlds such as Second Life or There.com, what these virtual worlds have in common is a built-in monetary exchange and economy that functions parallel to ones in everyday life and a call to create and complete some version of a task in order to reap rewards and win. As Greta Lorge states in her "Virtual Lessons, Real Productivity" article for Stanford, "Objects of value in these fantasylands elicit the same response that real money might: people want more." According to Stanford communication professor Byron Reeves, interviewed for the same article, these virtual-world pursuits are analogous to "real-world work: perform well, get a reward."

For Mashable blogger, Mark Dykeman, social media and MMORPG (including gaming and Second Life, There.com alike) have several similar characteristics which boil down the simple human pursuit of being social. Says Dykeman in his post *MMORPG Gamers and Social Media Junkies More Alike Than You'd Think*, "both pursuits have a social component. They allow people from different cities, countries, ethnic backgrounds, and other demographic categories to interact. You learn a lot by interacting with people, even if it's over the web. Good friendships have been made through both pursuits, sometimes culminating in real-life friendships and romantic relationships whether it's via Facebook, Twitter, or a Ning group – the same can happen in games. Both games and social media sites also allow us to maintain existing relationships when friends move away . . . You can also use both types of applications to explore worlds, real or imagined, as a way to satisfy creative, recreational, and social needs."

Back in Second Life, Linden Lab claims to have over 15 million totally unique residents as of early September 2008. While the total is certainly impressive, the same statistics presented by Linden Lab reveals that under 900,000 users have logged in within a given 30 days, and it's also worth noting that many of the "registered users" are duplicate accounts bringing the actual numbers of "active users" to approximately 550,000 people who are in-world an average of 40 hours a month (as of late Spring 2008) according to Second Life author and blogger, Wagner James Au.

Second Life by far provides the most in-depth statistics and analysis of their in-world economy. According to their blog reports, December 2007 revealed 893,000 residents were logged in for approximately 25.6 million user hours, averaging 30 hours a month per user. Of those residents, 519,000 (at the time) were deemed "active" residents meaning a user who was in-world for over an hour during the month. The active residents account for 25.5 million hours in-world, which averages out to 49 hours per month. According to Second Life's official blog, active residents spent more than US$0.30 per hour used. Per Second Life, "Most of this economic activity went to the more than 50,000 residents generating what we call 'positive monthly Linden dollar flow' from their activities in Second Life. We believe that many of these 50,000 users are creating the diverse creations and experiences that make Second Life such an interesting place to explore. This is the powerful engine fueling the steady long-term growth of Second Life. The growth in Q4 combined with continued growth in January demonstrates that the Second Life growth engine is alive and well." Of their users, Second Life reports US, France, Germany, the UK, and the Netherlands as the top five countries of origin. Although Second Life keeps country by country statistics, it still treats its users and marketers as internationally integrated versus Habbo, a highly successful world for teens, which divides both users and advertisers by country.

In 2008, the total number of user-to-user transactions, a measure of the gross domestic product in Second Life, grew by 14.3% to US$338 million from Q1 to Q2. The financial statistics for resident spending bumped up to US$0.87 per user hour, according to statistics released in Second Life's economy blog.

As of April 2008, Reuters, however reported that "Fewer new users are signing up for Second Life, but the faithful are spending more time and money than ever inside Linden Lab's virtual world" with the in-world economy growth rate of 15 percent annually, according to Linden Lab CFO John Zdanowski (a.k.a. Zee Linden in Second Life). While new users and premium subscriptions may be down, land transactions are up by 44% as of July 2008. "Because land represents nearly 8 times more revenue to us than premium accounts, our focus has been on the launching of new land products rather than on enhancing the premium subscription," stated Zdanowski in Second Life's economy blog.

TWEEN USER PROFILES AND HABITS

Parks Associates, a consumer and industry research firm specializing in consumer-oriented technology, presented the following statistics on users at the Virtual Worlds Conference 2007:

- 6% of US broadband users visit virtual worlds on a weekly basis;
- 18% have tried a virtual world at least once;
- Second Life is the number one virtual world visited, followed by virtual worlds for teens and kids;
- regular virtual-world's users often visit more than one virtual world.

On the youth side, the second Global Habbo Youth Survey found that 58,486 teens between the ages 11 and 18 from 31 countries could essentially be put into five categories:

- **Achievers:** Ambitious, strong minded and materialistic. They value material success and while having lots of friends,

24

they do not consider other people's feelings as much as other segments.

- **Rebels:** Value gathering lots of experiences in life and enjoy a fast-paced lifestyle. Like Achievers they want to become "rich and famous", but they are not willing to compromise on having fun in order to achieve this goal.
- **Traditionals:** Value having an ordinary life and see themselves as honest, polite and obedient. They are keen to help others but are less ambitious and pleasure seeking compared to other segments.
- **Creatives:** Share many of the same positive traits as Traditionals, but with a focus on creativity. They place value in getting a good education and being influential in life, but they are also active, social and have an interest in traveling.
- **Loners:** They are more introverted and less likely than other segments to identify with any specific personality traits. They rarely see themselves as active or self-assured, but are more open minded in their attitudes compared to Traditionals or Achievers.

While virtual worlds are by definition a social network, clearly virtual worlds and social media networks are two very different beasts. The success of MySpace, Facebook and even micro-blogging environments such as Twitter reflect this in the number of users compared to virtual worlds. Again according to Parks Associates, 40% of 25- to 34-year-olds actually participate in social networks but only 12% use virtual worlds. Of 18- to 24-year-olds, 71% participate in social networks, but only 10% use virtual worlds. Broken down by sex, 35% of females participate in social networks but only 5% females participate in virtual worlds. With males 29% participate in social networks while only 7% participate in virtual worlds.

While the numbers are relatively small with early adopters, the estimated growth is really quite staggering. At the Virtual

Worlds Conference 2007, another presenter Nic Mitham, managing director of K-Zero and a growth forecaster of virtual worlds, predicted the following rise in vw users from Q4 2007 to Q4 2008:

- Second Life 10 mn to 20 mn;
- There.com 1 mn to 7 mn;
- Kaneva 0.6 mn to 3 mn;
- HiPiHi 0 mn to 10 mn;
- Whyville 3 mn to 10 mn; and
- Club Penguin 15 mn to 30 mn.

Most of the growth, Mitham cites, is from kids growing up and migrating to other worlds and other markets opening further, specifically Western Europe, Russia, Eastern Europe, South America, and Asia. One audience segment that is conspicuously absent, notes Mitham, are Baby Boomers. It will likely take much easier interfaces and relevant activities to attract Boomers in higher numbers.

There.com and Second Life may battle it out as the top two contenders for adult virtual worlds, but as users go, There.com is geared towards a slightly younger age profile than Second Life with an average age of 22, which is 10+ years younger than the average Second Life users. To match its target age demographic, There.com positions itself more as a "hang-out" than a creative platform, although some content creation and proprietary currency (called "Therebucks") both exist. Likewise, newcomer Kaneva (which as of Spring 2008 is still in Beta) is initially targeting an equal gendered, 18-to-34 year old demographic and avoiding the under-18'ers all together. Like the other worlds, active users are already skewing towards more female than male, reported to be due to a predominance on activities like decorating and shopping and perhaps also due to the "MySpace-like" profiles created by residents, including the ability for streaming media. (The actual 3D environments are technically separate from the profiles/ streaming media.) Second Life also differs by having a minimum user age of 18 years old, while There.com allows 13 and up. According to K-Zero, a UK-based virtual-world's agency, 32% of registered There.com users are 13- to 17-years old. Second Life offers a Teen Second Life as well "to make friends and to play, learn and create" but no in-world economy exists, and the teen world is kept entirely separate from the adult one. (Although frankly it's hard to account for people of all ages who lie about their age.)

KIDS AND TWEEN WORLDS

The growth of virtual worlds specifically designed for the younger tweens and kids is staggering. As of Fall 2008, the number of youth-oriented worlds currently available is reported to be more than 60 with over 40 more going Beta shortly. Thanks to the success of Neopets (covered later in Chapter 4) and Club Penguin (which Disney ultimately bought for US$700 million) kids, tweens and teens are all the rage for targeted virtual worlds. Why? It breaks down to three simple factors:

1. Their purchasing power (of the reported US$ 51 billion spent by tweens in 2007, an additional $170 billion was spent by parents and family members directly for them, according to 360Youth.com).
2. Their natural prowess with learning new technologies.
3. They embrace brands and are highly loyal compared to brand-fickle older users.

One of the ways virtual worlds, kids and retailers are mixing is through real-life toy products that have a virtual-world tie-in.

(Films, books, and TV shows; other real-world entertainment properties are also adopting this model.) As companies took notice of the phenomenal success of Neopets and Webkinz (which offers a similar adopt-a-pet theme produced by plush toy maker Ganz), toy makers began tying real-world toys to online experiences like gang-busters. Russ's Shining Stars, Bratz dolls, Build-A-Bear, Ty's Beanie Babies 2.0, and Hasbro's Littlest Pet Shop VIPs are among the more recent entries into the space as of 2008. All toys come with some version of a "secret code" that is used to register online within the accompanying virtual world for further avatar customization, mini-games (i.e., games within games) and typically some form of social networking – from chat rooms to Facebook/MySpace-style profiles.

The folks running these worlds also work hard to engage parents as well particularly regarding online safety concerns. BarbieGirls.com with close to 11 million users since its recent launch reaches out to mothers in particular. Also in 2008, Disney announced it would be launching up to 10 virtual worlds based on even more refined age and demographic criteria and interests. While Club Penguin remains a huge success under its domain for ages as young as four years old, Toontown is mediocre numbers wise and Disney's Virtual Magic Kingdom targeted at tweens/early teens closed altogether in Spring 2008. That's not to say, the Virtual Magic Kingdom closed quietly, or that the few thousand loyal users didn't care. Blog rants, angry emails and a real-life demonstration outside Disney headquarters were all reported in the few short weeks since Disney announced it was lights out for the world.

To put some perspective on the growing bevy of pint-sized virtual worlds, Steve Youngwood, EVP of digital media at Nickelodeon/MTVN Kids and Family Group commented about Nickelodeon's own projects in Spring 2008, "There is no 'one size fits all' business model for our virtual worlds.

Each virtual world will be distinct and our approach to the business model should align with the goals for the user experience. We expect to see a mix of models throughout our virtual studio pipeline including advertising, premium services, and real-world product extensions." Between advertising, premium services and real-world product extensions, relevant brands to these worlds have plenty of opportunities to be active and present in a variety of ways.

While looking over Parks Associates' break downs of virtual world versus social networking numbers may not seem very impressive, keep in mind that these new frontiers are in general only growing. Michael Cai, director Broadband and Gaming at Parks Associates, estimated that in 2008 6 million to 8 million users will try out a virtual world and that 2 million to 3 million of those people will become weekly active users. That accounts for plenty of people steering the Internet in a whole new direction.

Sources

Disney, available from: http://news.idg.no/cw/art.cfm?id=12F8C3F5-17A4-0F78-3128E847501E9A30

Habbo, available from: http://www.clickz.com/showPage.html? page=3629026

Habbo Global Survey, available from: http://www.sulake.com/press/releases/2008-04-03-Global_Habbo_Youth_Survey.html

Kaneva.com, available from: http://www.digitalartsonline.co.uk/news/index. cfm?newsid=7369

Lorge, G. (2008) "Virtual Lessons, Real Productivity" in Stanford, A Publication of the Stanford Alumni Association, Jan/Feb: 53. Mary Gordon, available from: http://freshtakes.typepad.com/sl_communicators/2008/01/nine-questions.html

Mashable, available from: http://mashable.com/2008/09/05/gamers-and-social-media-users/Michael Cai, available from: http://www.mixedrealities.com/?p=117

Number of tween/kids worlds, available from: http://www.kzero.co.uk/blog/?cat=86

Parks Associates User Statistics, available from: http://www.sentient services.com/blog/2007/10/demographics-in-viritual-worlds-numbers.html

Platoni, K. (2008) "Seeing Is Believing" in Stanford, A Publication of the Stanford Alumni Association, Jan/Feb: 48–55.

Reuters on SL Economy, available from: http://secondlife.reuters.com/ stories/2008/04/15/sl-posts-strong-economic-growth-on-dwindling-enrollments/

Second Life Economic Statistics, available from: http://blog.secondlife. com/category/economy/

Steve Youngwood/Nickelodeon, available from: http://www.clickz.com/ show Page.html?page=3629026

Taran, available from: http://www.knowprose.com/node/18838Teen Second Life, available from: http://teen.secondlife.com/whatis

There.com vs. Second Life users, available from: http://www.kzero.co. uk/blog/ ?p=961

Tween purchasing power, available from: http://www.brandchannel. com/features_effect.asp?pf_id=284

Virtual World Toy Tie-Ins, available from: http://www.brandchannel. com/ start1.asp?fa_id=430

Wagner James Au, available from: http://www.businessweek.com/ technology/content/may2008/tc2008054_665274.htm

3

THE EMERGENCE OF BUSINESS WITHIN VIRTUAL WORLDS

"The risks businesses face as a result of getting involved in virtual worlds can be significant. These risks shouldn't be ignored, but neither should the potential opportunities and benefits that arise from using these new environments for corporate collaboration and communications."
—*Steve Prentice, Gartner Consulting Vice President*

WHY USE VIRTUAL WORLDS?

Aside from the fact the press has a love/hate relationship with them and advertising/media agencies are mesmerized by the marketing potential, at the end of the day, why should businesses step one digitally altered toe into virtual worlds? The key to 3D virtual worlds is that you are having live, face-to-face experiences whether it be with people or architecture or things that, while graphically "cartoonish" in nature, are surprisingly much more real life and human like. The fact that businesses can put their brand name on to products, games and experiences in virtual worlds so that real-life people via avatars can interact with that brand experientially and go beyond a single messaged, 2D ad is in essence what compels businesses to be there in the first place.

As Jennifer McLean, Director of Marketing for Double Fusion, an in-game advertising company put it in my original article on virtual world branding for Brandchannel.com, "By being three-dimensional and interactive, brands can move past the 'show me' paradigm of other media and get into the 'touch me' world of true interaction, which offers significantly more bandwidth for communication and for the transference of brand attributes."

A report by Forrester Research in April of 2008 marks enterprise spending on Web 2.0 technologies across North America, Europe and Asia over the next 5 years, growing 43% each year to reach $4.6 billion globally by 2013. According to Forrester, large businesses are as of April 2008 spending more on "employee collaboration tools than customer-facing Web 2.0 technologies." However, the research group expects this trend to reverse by 2009 and by 2013, "the investment in customer-facing Web 2.0 technology will dwarf spending on internal collaboration software by nearly a billion dollars."

TYPES OF BUSINESSES WITHIN VIRTUAL WORLDS

While some critics claim that the best a company can hope for is a bit of advertising and PR from a virtual world presence, in reality there are far more opportunities that are extended to a brand by being in world. Some brands are present not as much for the PR buzz as much as a means to reach out and communicate with specific audiences they want to reach, such as high tech companies reaching out to software developers.

As adult virtual world users grow in their numbers, more and more of the "mainstream" are coming into these worlds and are much less brand aversive than early adopters. Young audiences down to children are of course some of the most brand-oriented and accepting in-world – because, well, that's just how they are in real life. Like all mediums, though, good branding entirely depends on commitment levels, creativity and thinking outside the box to take advantage of beyond the virtual "brand placement" effect. Good branding also means tapping into passion (consumers' and branders' alike) in a similar way Hollywood taps into passionate fans.

At the 2007 Virtual Worlds Conference, Mary Ellen Gordon of Market Truths, an online market research agency, told attendees that the highest awareness levels of brands (i.e., brands mentioned unaided) in Second Life fall into five categories: information technology, athletic shoes, soft drinks, cars, and media.

Gordon also presented the following consumer behavior numbers:

- 57% considered buying a real-life product as a result of a recommendation they received from someone in Second Life;
- 55% recommended a real-life product to someone they were chatting to in Second Life;
- 25% have gone to look at a product in real life after seeing it in Second Life;
- 9% have purchased a product in real life after seeing it in Second Life;
- 8% have bought a real life product in Second Life.

Early on, the brands getting the most recognition from outside the sacred virtual world boundaries (via the press) were in some cases brands most people are never likely to have associated with such forward thinking technology. But before we go there, let's look a little further back.

Back in 2001, economist Edward Castronova wrote a paper on online game and virtual world economies half in jest. Castronova recounted to *Businessweek* for a 2006 article about meeting with Second Life along with journalist Julian Dibbell, Stanford University law professor and author Larry Lessig, and venture capitalists Jed Smith and Mitch Kapor in April 2003, where they talked about user-created content. "What we told them [Second Life] was that ownership, and the ability to liquidate the value of your virtual holdings, would in theory spark economic development. If you let people capture the value of what they create, they're going to create a lot more."

Apparently Linden Lab was listening and heeded the advice to change from a taxation-based socialist economic model (so to speak) to a capitalist free market in which users paid Linden Lab for land as well as the right to build what they wanted. The users could then charge other users for products, services and things to do – in other words virtual businesses were born.

It didn't take too long for large businesses to catch wind of virtual world economic potentials thanks to the "heads up" from media agencies. Castranova cites Second Life's embracement of commercialization as a part of its "core plan." As he told *Businessweek*, "It would be really bad for Second Life to be closed off from the real economy. It's a big part of its raison d'être, to be an economic space that is well-integrated into the real economy. That's different from a fantasy world [such as War of the Worlds]."

Leo Burnett, the global ad powerhouse agency, and its portfolio of smaller boutique agencies were among the earlier agencies to solicit big brands into virtual places. Because online gaming campaigns have offered brands attractive opportunities for very targeted advertising/marketing for a while, the leap into virtual worlds was not that large a stretch. What was interesting, however, from a brand marketer perspective was that some of the brands eager to go into these new realms were not necessarily the ones one would equate with ground-breaking technology.

For Leo Burnett Detroit, the idea of branding its first world client Pontiac, the less-than-top-of-mind American car brand on Second Life, came from a collaborative partnership formed with a viral marketing agency called Campfire. Burnett Detroit was already following the developments of Second Life and began to take note of some very early trendsetter marketers in this burgeoning virtual world, including the success of Adidas as an early entrant to Second Life, with its virtual store and exclusive "A3 Microride" (see Screenshot 3A) that were designed by virtual world agency River Runs Red to fit avatar feet perfectly giving him/her/it a walk with "bounce and flexibility" for a mere 50 Linden Dollars or approximately US$0.19.

According to Leo Burnett's spokesperson, involvement in Second Life seemed "a perfect fit" for Pontiac's marketing strategy, citing Pontiac's preference of a fusion marketing approach

SCREENSHOT 3A   Adidas A3 Microride
Source: River Runs Red

using non-traditional marketing tactics to engage consumers. Pontiac was already lending its brand name to staging impromptu concerts with popular rock bands in New York's Times Square to gaming, creating the Pontiac Virtual NCAA Final 4 (PVNF4) program, which according to Burnett, made them one of the first marketers to leverage multiple media opportunities inside and around a videogame (College Hoops 2K6).

The chance to interact directly with its target audience in a way that encouraged "curiosity and familiarity" with the brand was a direct appeal. "Everyone would assume that if a user is excited enough to purchase a virtual version of a Pontiac, that it might be something that rubs off in the real world."

Using Castronova, Dibbell, Lessig, Smith and Kapor's model of buying land to create opportunities for commerce, Pontiac and Leo Burnett created "Motorati Island" (see Screenshot 3B) complete with fantasy Pontiac race cars (dubbed the Pontiac Solstice GXP) and tracks to race them on, as well as the now popular strategy of creating a live music stage and forum for fans. Inspired by its endorsement of Times Square live rock concerts, the Pontiac Second Life camp recruited heavy weight performer Jay-Z for one of its concerts. Due to the common problems both then and now of poor sound quality caused by lag and a maximum capacity of 100 avatars able to attend, the concert was not without its problems. Fortunately for Pontiac, what would have been unforgivable technical problems in the real world became common and fairly overlooked problems in the virtual one. Unfortunately for Pontiac, despite decent community activity, their stay within Motorati Island eventually came to an end at the end of 2007 when the company made the decision to pull out of Second Life after spending what has been described as "too much money to sustain." Pontiac and their agencies never gave an exact reason for departing.

SCREENSHOT 3B   Pontiac Motorati Island

The list of companies who have tried or are still trying out virtual worlds and Second Life in particular is vast and varied across industries/sectors (see Screenshot 3B2). NASA, NOAA (National Oceanic and Atmospheric Administration), IBM, Sun, Cisco, AMD, Amazon, Best Buy, Jean-Paul Gaultier, BBC, MTV, Duran Duran, Reuters, Playboy, Coca-Cola, CNN, Geek Squad, Herman Miller, Bantam Dell, CareerBuilder.com, H&R Block, real-life governments and embassies such as those representing Sweden (see Screenshot 3C) and Estonia, and real-life universities such as Stanford, Ball State and Pepperdine are to name just a few.

While technology companies may be the usual suspects for virtual worlds, other brands within travel, education and government are among the not-so-usual. To date several countries are represented within Second Life including the United States for reasons that are as varied as their nation branding tactics: from Sweden's effort to "enshrine the country's reputation as

SCREENSHOT 3B2   Rasmusson Foundation Event in Second Life

SCREENSHOT 3C   Second House of Sweden

an innovative and forward thinking locale" through its Second Life Swedish Embassy to the Tuscan Tourist Foundation's virtual tours of the Tower of Pisa and the Ponte Vecchio in Italy that also directs visitors to an e-commerce site to buy real world souvenirs and so on. As Dan Herman of Wikinomics puts it, "So whether you're a possible investor looking for

SCREENSHOT 3D NOAA (National Oceanic and Atmospheric Administration)

information about the taxation of expats, or a tourist looking for visa info, these new [government] outposts [are] an additional source."

Of the US governmental agencies with a presence on Second Life, the National Oceanic and Atmospheric Administration (NOAA) has the most robust facility contained with in its own island, called Meteora (see Screenshot 3D). Virtual visitors can experience a hurricane on the wing of a research aircraft, rise through the atmosphere clinging to a weather balloon, stand on a beach during a tsunami, or ride underwater on a NOAA submersible. The way the weather and atmospheric wonderland was developed (managed by the agency's Earth System Research Laboratory) actually followed a common trend within Second Life in particular: by holding a competition among Second Life design companies and letting Second Life residents help choose the winner. (Herman Miller, Coca-Cola and countless others have also used the user design and judge contest concept to create branded content in world.)

Along with governmental agencies, virtual worlds have quickly become a popular and rather fascinating place for e-learning and top tier universities. According to Linden Lab at least 300 universities around the world teach classes or conduct research in Second Life and many on There.com. From dissecting virtual frogs to exploring complicated 3D models to debating technology patent law, the reasons for universities being in virtual worlds, like the government agencies, are varied yet highly practical. Students from all around the world versus a local campus gather regularly to use the virtual worlds as a learning center, laboratory, place for simulations and virtual field trips as well as a good old-fashioned place to chat and hang out. The California University's Davis School of Medicine was reported in 2007 to use Second Life as a forum to recreate for others the experience of a paranoid hallucination as experienced by a schizophrenic person. Associate Dean and Professor of Geography at the University of New Orleans Merrill Johnson cited perhaps the most practical reason of all for a university to employ virtual world models, telling *U.S. World & News Report* earlier this year, "If there were another disaster like [hurricane] Katrina, this would be a first resort. The virtual campus would still be intact. Even though students might be in Maine, California, and Texas, they could still gather in the virtual conference room and have some real-time communication."

As another unlikely contender, H&R Block has managed to not only be in Second Life, but receive real-life kudos for doing so. In 2007, Computer World magazine named H&R Block Island one of the eight "most useful corporate sites within Second Life." Conceived in 2006, H&R Block's island features tax offices for real-life IRS tax questions, an auditorium, product pavilion and a well-lit dance floor with DJ (see

SCREENSHOT 3E   H&R Block

Screenshot 3E). Avatars can receive a script made (or at least branded) by H&R Block to dance the tango out on the H&R dance floor. "Tango" also happens to be the name of their new online tax preparation product retailing for US$70.

For MTV the push to virtual worlds and the creation of its own proprietary worlds (see Chapter Five) is all about being a market leader. As the company who defined a new media genre with music video television, cross marketing to other visual mediums through what it calls its "4D" cross platform strategy (essentially content from MTV Networks' television shows loaded into 3D virtual worlds to create viewer feedback and experience) is a natural transition.

Along the same entertainment lines, a small San Francisco-based boutique agency called This Second Marketing created an avatar-oriented promotion for the IMAX version of the *Harry Potter Order of the Phoenix* film in 2007. An IMAX executive reported to the *Hollywood Reporter* trade magazine, "A huge proportion of our opening weekend tickets came from advance Internet purchases, and a large number of those people came from interacting on Second Life."

For yet other innovators in their field such as the ever-effusive Jean-Paul Gaultier (perhaps best known for Parisian couture and crafting Madonna's boobs into sharp objects), being the first to virtual worlds is as much an artistic statement as it is a commercial one. Jean-Paul Gaultier launched his 2007 "Fleur du Male" fragrance within an all-white, sculpturally based backdrop within Second Life. According to Emmanuel Vivier of Vanksen Buzz & Communication Agency based in Luxembourg, the operation was the brainchild of a former colleague named Galienni and "was very successful in terms of PR," citing it as one of the first cosmetics and luxury brands to used SL. Vivier commented, "JPG did a smart move by innovating while not going to SL for the sake of it. Instead of creating a year long presence with poor activity, they created a temporary, finely designed space for the [perfume's] launch event." To mitigate any PR risks, JPG "carefully selected" an invitee list of influential bloggers and SLers, giving them access to the party only via a code. To make it more viral, avatars received a white flower that they could wear on their virtual attire.

STRATEGIES AND TACTICS FROM REAL WORLD BRANDS

In its news blog IBM proclaimed in 2007, "To IBM, today's virtual worlds like Second Life and World of Warcraft are *simply a glimpse of the future Web*, with the same potential to transform business and society as the first waves of the web." Initial virtual world business uses for Big Blue are described as for "enhanced training, immersive social-shopping experiences, simulations for learning and rehearsing business processes, and event hosting." A spokesman for IBM said it has never approached virtual worlds from a strictly marketing strategy for, but rather as one to help other businesses optimize their own presence in-world. Sears and Circuit City are two retail clients that IBM created soup to nuts storefronts for within Second Life (see Screenshot 3F). In 2008, Linden Lab and IBM began creating the ultimate firewall to allow employees to collaborate without fear of prying outside eyes. It was announced the two companies were exploring the development of enterprise solutions for security-rich, custom virtual world creation and collaboration on the Second Life Grid platform. While there are reported to be more than 100 corporate "storefronts" in Second Life, none apparently employ a firewall. As a result of the firewall, IBM employees can work together in a secured

SCREENSHOT 3F   IBM

Second Life area (no matter where they are in the world) and when they're finished, may exit their area to join the rest of the general Second Life experience. IBM worked with Linden Lab to pilot a solution internally, that was designed to allow IBM employees to explore the Second Life mainland and seamlessly cross over into IBM's custom-built world behind the firewall without having to log on and off. The goal is to allow IBM employees to access public spaces and private spaces within one Second Life client interface while privatizing and securing portions of the Second Life Grid behind IBM's firewall. As of early summer 2008, the IBM/Second Life collaboration is still in prototype mode.

For some companies, the cross into virtual worlds is a literal one. Crowne Plaza Hotels, owned by the Intercontinental Hotel Group is one such brand that has crossed its real world brick and mortar buildings that temporarily house business travelers and host private business meetings with PowerPoint slide presentations on a screen to a virtual building that also hosts private business meetings with PowerPoint slide presentations (see Screenshot 3G). Food, hot coffee and one-way mirrors for observing market research panels are also in the virtual version. Security (or is that Ecurity?) is present at every level of the virtual Crown Plaza where meeting spaces can only be entered by the actual attendees, and avatars are politely "ejected" out of the meeting room once the meeting's time is up. Outside the facilities, Coca-Cola offers its "Virtual Thirst" vending machines (covered in the next chapter) for virtual breaks.

Del Ross, VP of Distribution Marketing, Americas for Crowne Plaza Hotels told Cybergrrl Oh (a.k.a. girl-power web pioneer Aliza Sherman) in her Second Life Business show that the company made a "cautious moderate investment" into SL. "We're the largest hotel company in the world and spend hundred of millions of dollars on marketing – this is considered

SCREENSHOT 3G   Crowne Plaza Hotels

more of a medium size campaign for this venture." Ross goes on to cite the company's SL raison d'être as a means to "increase awareness of Crowne Plaza Hotels brand and its value proposition with the meeting space." Media placement and media hits are important factors to the company and Ross is "pleased with the results." Ross reports that Crowne's in-world presence received 30 million PR impressions (print, TV, web) in the first 9 months following the launch of the service. In addition, a meeting takes place on Place to Meet island nearly every day.

Whether or not the grand experiment in virtual worlds is worth it is, for some companies, debatable. As Ken Wohlrob, Director of Internet Marketing for book publisher Bantam Dell told Aliza Sherman on her SL Business show when she asked, "Is SL worth it?" Wohlrob replied, "Yes and no – the experiment is great. I think something else is coming along that will be better. It's kind of like a first generation iPod. . . . Consider SL like Yahoo! back in the day. It seemed like a great thing and then Google came along and just trounced Yahoo! I think there will be an even better virtual world or even one spot where you can access all virtual worlds. But I think it's a great experiment and interesting and that's why we're doing it. We consider the experiment important enough to what comes next that it's worth the time being in here [SL]."

On the youth side, virtual worlds for pre-schoolers, kids/ tweens, and teens in particular have enjoyed great success and are currently looked upon favorably even by the analysts. In 2008, JP Morgan released its "Nothing But Net: 2008 Internet Investment Guide" as a 312 page overview and analysis of Internet-based investments including virtual worlds. The company divides virtual worlds into "two audiences, two differing growth curves" meaning children's worlds and worlds aimed at adults. The latter, which it defines as being in its "infancy," but states, it will in 2008 experience "rapid growth." What JP Morgan is actually bullish on are kid's worlds stating that they "present parents an opportunity to let their kids play online and interact in a closed environment that is perceived as safe, especially when sites are operated by companies with trusted brands." For an example of a children's world see Screenshot 3H.

With the successful marriage of retail toy products and virtual worlds á la Webkinz, Neopets, Barbie.com and others (covered in the next chapter), virtual worlds for children have made other toy manufacturers take notice and join in on the trend as a way to growth to augment rather stagnant toy sales over the last few years. According to research by the Toy Industry Association Inc., a New York City-based trade group, toy sales totaled $22.3 billion in 2006, but youth electronics was the only industry segment to gain more than 5%. Many segments saw decreases, including action figures and accessories, down 9%.

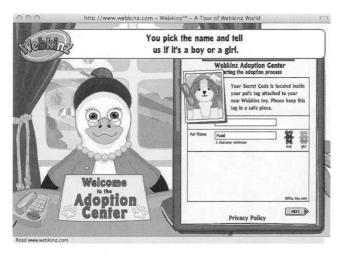

SCREENSHOT 3H   Webkinz

Tying real world toys to online experiences, the toys come with some version of a "secret code" that is used to register within the accompanying virtual world full of avatar customization, mini-games and some form of social networking from chat rooms to Facebook/MySpace-style "profiles" that are shared with other users. Russ's Shining Stars (plush animals), Bratz dolls, Ty's Beanie Babies 2.0, and Hasbro's Littlest Pet Shop VIPs are among the more recent entries into the space as of 2008. Citing an eMarketer report from September, JP Morgan believes that half of all kids will visit virtual worlds by 2011.

Habbo (formerly Habbo Hotel), the largest virtual world for teens (see Screenshot 3I), knows as well the popularity of virtual worlds and brands. After surveying over 50,000 youths around the world on brand preferences, spending habits, and other topics in its second Global Habbo Youth Survey, the study found that 58,486 teens between the ages 11 and 18 from 31 countries do not find social networks as high a priority as imagined by big business and even the press.

SCREENSHOT 3I   Habbo

Emmi Kuusikko, Director of User and Market Insight for Sulake, Habbo's parent company, commented that, "Perhaps surprisingly social networks [such as Facebook, MySpace, etc.] appear as relatively low online priorities for young people, as 40 per cent of teens *do not view social networks as an important part of their online* experience on a global basis. This is due to the English-language bias of most social networks but considering Habbo's global success this also suggests that the localization of sites is important for teens communicating online. In countries where social networks are considered popular though they have become a regular communication channel between friends." As of the end of 2007, 70% of Habbo users are between the ages of 13 and 16, and according to Comscore registered avatars were up to the 80 million mark with 2.4 million unique visitors per month.

Back to the brand side of things, Habbo's survey showed that brand familiarity does, however, direct teens' choices as consumers, with 74% of those surveyed stating that familiar brands guide their purchasing decisions. Given that many virtual worlds for youth are still heavily girl-skewed in their user bases, it's interesting to note that McDonald's, Coca-Cola, Nike and Nokia ranked high for both boys and girls within the survey with gender differences being more visible in clothing brands, such as Adidas and Billabong as top boy brands and Hennes & Mauritz (H&M) and Roxy as top girl choices.

To make the most of teens' natural affinity to big brands, Habbo leverages its virtual world for real world branding, such as for in-game billboards, contests, interstitials and instant-console messaging, customized brand rooms, and sponsored quests – all of which, the company claims, "create a natural integration that adds value and appeals to teens." In fact, Habbo capitalizes on tween/teen affinities to big brands as a part of everyday life. Over 200 brands around the world are reported to have advertised in, integrated with, or sponsored elements of the Habbo world. "Habbo is about real life," commented Teemu Huuhtanen, president of the North America region at Sulake, "Teens are expecting to see brands, and give us regular feedback."

There.com, geared for 13-year-olds and up, has seen its share of popularity with larger brands grow. Betsy Book, Director of Product Management for Makena Technologies/There.com, stated she's observed a growing trend of brands coming into There.com because of *other* brands. Book cites *CosmoGirl* magazine and its first virtual prom event in their CosmoGirl Village located within There.com as an example of brands converging to be in front of a highly enthusiastic avatar crowd and coming into There.com through the other brands involved. The magazine's partners for the event included ABC Family and ACUVUE Brand Contact Lenses. In addition to dancing, virtual corsages and a Virtual Prom

Queen and King competition, virtual prom activities included:

- video trailers for ABC Family's original reality series, "America's Prom Queen";
- avatar makeovers with colored contact lenses from ACU-VUE(R);
- photo opportunities on the virtual red carpet;
- free give-away prizes, such as a virtual tiara inspired by "America's Prom Queen."

The after-party was held in-world at the ACUVUE OASYS™ Lounge. Commenting on the convergence of real-life passions, brands and virtual play, Vicki Wellington, *CosmoGirl* Publisher stated, "Prom is a high school girl's biggest night of the year, and we wanted to find a way to celebrate in both the real world and the virtual world. A virtual prom enables us to offer cutting edge ways to engage our readers with the brands and events they love most."

The virtual prom concept was enough of a hit to inspire Kaneva.com to host its own virtual prom with Bravo TV's Project Runway 2008 designer winner, Christian Siriano designing virtual fashions for prom goers to purchase.

Book also stated that since Makena Technologies (creator of There.com) partnered with *CosmoGirl* in November 2007 to extend its brand in-world, the CosmoGirl Village has become a highly popular place for girls 13 through college age to hang out. "They [*CosmoGirl*] just get virtual worlds and what they're about especially compared to other companies. It's sometimes hard to keep up with all of *their* ideas." Located along a coastal area in There.com, dance parties, fashion shows, spa makeovers, photo booths, live events, rich media and shopping for virtual- and real world clothing and accessories are among the village offerings. Thanks to the village's popularity with readers, advertisers with *CosmoGirl* off-line are warming up to in-world events. In 2008, Gillette Venus, Cover Girl, and Tampax Pearl came together to host a "Get Ready for Summer" event within the CG! Village. At the time of writing, *CosmoGirl* reached over 8 million teen readers.

Unfortunately for CosmoGirl, their positive virtual world experiences were not enough to keep the print version of the magazine from facing the hatchet. As of mid October 2008, Hearst Corp. announced it was shutting the doors on *CosmoGirl* by the end of the year (nine years since its spinoff from women's magazine *Cosmopolitan*) due to declining ad sales. Hearst also stated that *CosmoGirl* would "continue on the Internet as a part of the company's network of teen-focused Web sites."

Sources

CosmoGirl, available from: http://www.there.com/pr_cgprom.html; http://www.virtualworldsnews.com/2008/05/gaia-teams-with.html; http://www.virtualworldsnews.com/business/index.html;www.hearst.com/magazines/property/mag_prop_cosmogirl.html+number+of+readers+cosmogirl&hl=en&ct=clnk&cd=10&gl=us&client=firefox-a Wall Street Journal, "Hearst to Shutter CosmoGirl" by Shira Ovide, October 11–12, 2008

Crowne Plaza Hotels, available from: slcn.tv/real-biz-sl-crowne-plaza-hotels

Edward Castronova, available from: http://www.businessweek.com/magazine/content/06_18/b3982010.htm

Forrester Research, available from: http://www.govtech.com/gt/295682

Habbo, available from: http://www.sulake.com/press/releases/2008-04-07-Double-Fusion.html;http://www.clickz.com/showPage.html?page=3629026

Habbo Survey, available from: http://www.sulake.com/press/releases/2008-04-03-Global_Habbo_Youth_Survey.html

Harry Potter/IMAX, available from: http://www.businessweek.com/technology/content/may2008/tc2008054_665274.htm

H&R Block, available from: http://www.linuxinsider.com/story/virtualworlds/62476.html

IBM, available from: http://www.news.com/8301-10784_3-9730042-7.html; http://www.linuxinsider.com/story/virtual worlds/62447.html

Interviews with author: Aliza Sherman, January 2008; Emmanuel Vivier, May 2008; Betsy Book, May 2008

Jennifer McLean, available from: http://www.brandchannel.com/features_ effect.asp?pf_id=358

JP Morgan: http://www.virtualworldsnews.com/2008/01/jp-morgan-bulli.html

MTV, available from: http://www.news.com/MTV-goes-4D-with-virtual worlds- push/2100-1043_3-6171474.html

Number of Universities, available from: http://www.govtech.com/gt/252550? topic=118264

Pontiac and Leo Burnett Group, available from: http://www.brandchannel.com/ features_effect.asp?pf_id=358

Steve Prentice, available from: http://management.silicon.com/itdirector/ 0,39024673,39168101,00.htm

Swedish Embassy, available from: http://www.wikinomics.com/blog/index. php/2008/01/11/second-life-and-government/

Toy Industry Statistics, available from: http://209.85.173.104/search?q=cache: WbKzC2VAvLIJ:www.funosophy.com/fun/static/pdf/ChicagoTribune07052007.pdf+Russ+shining+stars+target+audience+age&hl=en&ct=clnk&cd=4&gl=us&client=firefox-a (Chicago Tribune)

University of California & Schizophrenia, available from: http://www.smh.com.au/news/biztech/look-whos-got-a-second-life/2006/12/05/1165080887728.html

University of New Orleans, available from: http://www.usnews.com/articles/education/e-learning/2008/01/10/a-second-life-for-higher-ed.html

4

THE VIRTUAL WORLDS OF PROPRIETARY BRANDS

STRATEGIES, TACTICS AND IMPACT OF VIRTUAL WORLDS BUILT AROUND A GLOBAL BRAND

> "Why co-mingle a brand like the NBA in a virtual world like Second Life when you can create your own virtual NBA world? We think we can attract 10 to 20 million mainstream consumers to a focused virtual world site and deliver a full brand experience."
> —*Michael Pole, Trilogy Studios CEO*

As discussed in the last chapter, big brands in virtual worlds may be a love/hate experiment for most, but it's one that is being explored more and more. Another element to a big brand's virtual strategy is to look into a world of its own. Of course this class of branded content is very much the exclusive domain of the über brands – Disney, Coke, Viacom, Sony, and as discussed in Chapter 2, it's increasingly directed around very specific (read young) target audiences. The result is the emergence of branded stand-alone virtual worlds that are a true convergence of gaming, entertainment, community, fantasy and commerce aimed specifically at young people aged from 24 down to 4.

While originally a brand with no awareness, one of the greatest success stories to become an über-brand in and of itself is Neopets. Dubbed as a virtual pet community, Neopets debuted back in 1999 as a website for kids where children created a Neopet as a personal companion to dress and care for while exploring the Neopets' homeland of Neopia. By 2004, the site was reported to tens of millions of members with over 108 million pets. Taking notice of its massive commercial success worldwide, Viacom stepped in and bought the company in 2005 for US$160 million and relaunched the site in 2007 as a more sophisticated "Neopets 2.0" version. According to Nickelodeon, Neopets now boasts "54 species of Neopets, 16 lands, hundreds of characters, stories and plotlines, 200 games, a virtual economy based on 'Neopoints', daily and weekly creativity contests, Neovision™ video player, discussion boards, quests, and virtual items to collect, and most recently, NC Mall™," where users can purchase upscale tchotchkes for their pets. With 44 million registered members worldwide, the virtual world is now available in 11 languages and is the largest global kid-focused virtual world as of 2008. Its success, as well as success in the children's vw marketplace, in general has encouraged Nickelodeon to spend $100 million as of 2008 to develop more worlds.

The Neopets branded virtual world became a posterchild for the successful marriage between technology-adaptive kids and toys and entertainment, and as of 2008 is the largest global youth-focused virtual world. The average length of time per user on the site per month is 2 hours and 45 minutes, according to Comscore. With its 2008 launch of a new toy line and trading cards, that time may indeed go up. Each and every toy sold comes with exclusive virtual prize codes to redeem in-world. Webkinz and as of 2008, Beanie Babies 2.0 are other similar virtual pet worlds.

DISNEY'S TOONTOWN

The early success of Neopets was not lost on Disney as well. Although never one to shy away from technology it has never been known for fully adapting and employing it well. In 2003, the entertainment giant decided to develop Toontown massively multiplayer online (MMO) game aimed squarely for North American kids. It later arrived in Britain and France in 2004, with the European versions enjoying a major facelift in including more community content by the Walt Disney Internet Group in 2007.

As I wrote for an article on *Brandchannel*, Disney's Toontown is a spin off of its 1988 half animated/half live-action film "Who Framed Roger Rabbit." A trip to your nearest Disney theme park presents Toontown as fun, cartoon-inspired, life-sized sculptures of houses, shops, street lights and signs that kids and adults alike can enter and interact with. The technological version of Toontown takes this same idea but applies it to the web á la Second Life, offering a multiplayer, online 3D game designed for kids and families.

Because it's Disney and designed for kids, the content (to the relief of most parents) is highly sanitized and considered safe. Whereas much of online gaming these days include vast amounts of graphic violence (of varying degrees), Disney limits their "violence" to cartoon gags designed to crack up (quite literally) the humor-free robots known as Cogs who are out to turn the colorful, vibrant Toontown into a "corporate metropolis."

Like Second Life and other virtual world sites, players create and dress a Toon avatar to represent themselves in this virtual Disneyworld, explore neighborhoods, furnish their own place to live, design their own race karts, train a pet "Doodle" and, of course, team up with other players to defeat the devious Cogs. The game artwork is sophisticated 3D animation that gives the appearance of highly "computerized" versus the vibrant two-dimensional artwork and animation Disney is famous for.

There are also mini-games within the site such as Lucky Number, Underwater Ring and Match Minnie, which earns players jellybeans (the Toon version of money) to buy props from Goofy's Gag Shop that can be used in the ongoing battle with the Cogs. Unlike other virtual world sites, membership is not free with the exception of a free, three-day trial. Living and playing in Toontown costs £6.99 per month.

Despite some technical limitations, Toontown is slowly making its way around the world. Walt Disney Internet Group announced its arrival in South East Asia at the beginning of 2008. Since its North American launch in 2003, it has won several gaming and parents' awards and reported to have over 15 million unique Toon avatars as players – overall a modest number for one of the best-known brands.

As noted in Chapter 2, Disney is not without virtual world successes and failures in its portfolio. The company bought tween-haven Club Penguin in a US$700 million deal, which boasted 217 million unique worldwide users in May 2008 according to Comscore – a 17% increase from the year before. Disney has made its ownership mark known by superimposing the Disney name and logo just above Club Penguin and making it accessible through the Disney.com website. Despite the closure of their Virtual Magic Kingdom aimed at tweens (much to the chagrin of some die-hard fans), the company is fully committed to more and more virtual worlds that are highly targeted including Pirates of the Carribbean Online for tween boys and Pixie Hollow for younger girls, which create communities around the context of specific stories. The add-ons are apparently in response to watching successful trends in the market, with Pixie Hollow reported to be Disney's answer to Hello Kitty Online, the light-hearted branded virtual world aimed at girls featuring the world's most licensed white cat. The company believes that it is this context that will ultimately add value to both consumers and business. Warner Brothers Entertainment, part of Time Warner, seems to agree and is as of 2008 developing a series of worlds based on its Looney Tunes, Hanna-Barbera and D.C. comics properties.

Not to be left in the dust, toy maker Mattel and its iconic Barbie brand has also gone virtual with a retail twist. As of Spring 2008, Mattel enjoyed the fastest growing vw to date with its BarbieGirls.com, which combines a virtual world with a Barbie Doll MP3 player. Built by Studiocom, the same digital media agency responsible for Coke Studios, the site already had four million users after just a couple of months of its public beta run in 2007. While the world is free to play within, buyers of the MP3 accessory have access to its premium areas. By the printing of this book, Barbie.com will have abandoned the MP3 accessory and opened up the world to girls with good old cash. Entrance is free and basic actions like chatting, dressing up and decorating rooms are as well. But there will also be premium games and fashion that are open only to V.I.P. players, which requires a premium subscription. Barbie.com is not without its élitism by distinguishing the haves and have-nots by who has a sparkling tiara (V.I.P.) and who doesn't (free users).

Be-Bratz, the irreverent, highly successful competitor doll to Barbie, and its maker Hasbro has also followed Barbie's lead by offering Be-Bratz.com. Girls purchase a Be-Bratz doll in the usual retail store locations and then register in the companion virtual world with the USB "glam necklace" that comes with the toy. In addition to the doll and necklace, a mouse, mouse pad, small pet comes with the package for a retail price of US$29.99. Customization abounds in Be-Bratz and of course there are lots (and lots) of in-world shopping opportunities.

Lego, the Danish children's connector block kings, are looking to launch their own MMORPG aimed at the young set sometime soon as well. Dubbed Lego Universe, the world's different exploration areas has already been set up by the company, but users will come in and build, customize and create their environment and things with virtual Lego both individually and collectively as well as complete quests. Parents will be relieved to know that there is a zero chance for gratuitous blood, guts and gore since "mini-figures" (i.e., avatars) will simply break apart like real world Lego when killed or wounded.

Nic Mitham, head of KZero a virtual world consultancy based in the UK, explains the raison d'être of being in-world. "The motivation for these companies to create virtual playgrounds is simple – it's an extension of the real world toy play and keeps the children in a 'branded' frame of mind."

Again based on the numbers of users on just the worlds mentioned above, there is no doubt millions of kids are spending substantial time in virtual worlds and will continue to do so due to their mass acceptance. eMarketer predicts that by 2011 53% of all American child and teen Internet users will visit virtual worlds at least once a month. As kids/tween oriented brands crank up their volumes with branded stand-alone virtual worlds, teens and young adults are also prime audiences for the iconic brands that need no introduction.

COKE STUDIOS

MyCoke.com (then CokeMusic.com) and its original Coke Studios portion of the site came about in 2002 as one of the first consumer product websites to integrate a virtual world experience and boasted a reported 8 million registered users. Initially targeted at young people 13 and up within the US, Quantcast.com puts MyCoke.com numbers as reaching approximately 21,509 US monthly unique users catering to an upper income class (over US$100K household income), with a female skewed audience. Quantcast asserts that the typical user also visits teen virtual hang-out Habbo (formerly Habbo Hotel) and dressupgames.com.

SCREENSHOT 4A   Coke CC Metro in There.com

After 5 years of experimentation, Coke Studios gave way to CC Metro (see Screenshot 4A), a joint partnership launched in 2007 with Coke and Makena Technologies (the company behind There.com) to create a richer virtual world environment housed within There.com, offering all the usual young-person activity laundry list: music; gaming; sports; entertainment; exclusive videos presented by Coke; and even a skate park to hone virtual hoverboard skills – all within a "PG-13" environment. CC Metro appears as a classic contour bottle shaped "continent" within There.com, and Coca-Cola's partnerships with entertainment phenomenon such as American Idol, NASCAR and the 2008 Olympic Games in Beijing are all integrated as branded entertainment experiences within Coke's virtual world. CC Metro is accessible both through MyCoke. com and There.com (see Screenshot 4B.)

SCREENSHOT 4B   Coke CC Metro in There.com

Sony's PlayStation gaming empire has created community based- virtual world called "Home" that allows users to create an avatar for their PlayStation 3 console, and like teen world Habbo, gives users virtual apartments, clothing and décor for free and for purchase. Users also interact in the trophy room of the "Hall of Fame" where they can put on display their personal trophies for in-game achievements and real-time score rankings in PS3 games. According to Wikipedia, "Sony wants to give people the tools to create their own things, but they also want a safe place for younger users to feel comfortable."

vMTV

If by now you've noticed that some of the largest proprietary virtual worlds are owned and/or created by just a few companies, you've been paying attention. In addition to Viacom's successful Neopets, the cable television and entertainment

SCREENSHOT 4C   vMTV The Hills

behemoth also has virtual worlds for tweens with Nicktropolis (and is launching an entire virtual world based on *SpongeBob SquarePants*), and for teens and older with vMTV. vMTV is the official virtual MTV world fictitiously based in Southern California. Virtual dancing, socializing and making out at the bar are just a few highlights vMTV touts to visitors. As of 2008, what the world is primarily known for is its marriage of 2D cable TV content, online micro-sites and 3D virtual worlds creating what the company calls the "4D TV" or "multi-screen strategy" as a hybrid approach to media content. MTV's *Virtual Laguna Beach* and *Virtual Hills* (see Screenshot 4C) were among the first virtual worlds based on the content of TV shows and were created in partnership with Makena Technologies (the same folks for There.com and Coke's CC Metro). *The Real World*, *Pimp My Ride* and more were added later, and as of 2008, new shows-turned-worlds with a gaming twist are being added to capture more male audiences. To date, users/viewers of vMTV and its associated shows are skewed 65/35 female to male (the same as the show audiences the worlds are based on) according to *Virtual World News*. However, a company spokesman stated that the female to male ratio is more even at this point. What the company is focusing on as of early Summer 2008 is to launch a newer version of vMTV that will be the next phase of its evolution.

So what are these virtual world brand experiences doing for MTV? In addition to increased brand engagement and awareness, there is an increased likeliness that virtual commerce will translate into real world commerce. According to blogger Ravi Mehta, "Over 80% of the MTV Virtual Worlds' community has purchased a branded virtual good and these virtual goods have been used over 5 million times. And MTV has found that *people who purchased and used branded virtual goods have a radically increased interest in purchasing that brand's physical goods*." While no quantitative statistics could be found to substantiate this claim, it is quite plausible – a concept not lost on parents of children who want to buy as much of the real world toys, books, etc. associated with an entertainment experience as possible.

Related to this claim, MTV in the Spring of 2008 released results of a controlled study done with viewers of MTV show *The Hills* and Pepsi as an advertiser (see Screenshot 4D). Dubbed the "Multiscreen Engagement Case Study" and conducted for MTV by Harris Interactive and MauroNewMedia earlier in the year, the research studied a 300 person control group who did not watch *The Hills* and a 300 person control group who did watch the show. Of the 300 who watched the show, 80% (240 viewers), rated the program with a numerical score of 4 or 5, with 5 being the best score and 1 being the lowest. The majority of the study focused on these viewers who rated it a 4 or 5. Approximately 50% of the 240 fans who watched the show on television stated that "Pepsi promotes music events and supports music artists." Less than 30% stated

SCREENSHOT 4D   Pepsi in vMTV

the brand was "in touch with youth culture," and about 15% considered Pepsi "cool" or "hip." A small 1% felt Pepsi exposed viewers to the latest trends, styles and fashion. As a brand that prides itself on being associated with youth and cool trends, the numbers measured weren't exactly the most encouraging.

However, when these same users were interviewed for their responses to Pepsi *after* interacting in *The Hills* virtual world, the percentages shot up dramatically: *over 90%* stated Pepsi promotes music and recording artists, and nearly *70%* considered the brand to be "cool, hip, and in touch with youth culture."

Tim Rosta, MTVN's integrated marketing executive vice president gave his own analysis of the research outcomes: "What we've learned from the study is the more our audience engages with a brand across a platform the greater level of brand affinity they have. When we infuse it appropriately, brands become part of the dialog giving us the ability to create brand ambassadors. They know somebody is paying for the programming so they embrace brands where we don't try to fool them."

Just two years earlier, when Pepsi committed to MTV's first virtual world effort, the decision was "largely based on gut" versus research. An executive told *Adweek*, "There was nothing else on the market we felt good about, so we decided to test it with a trusted partner. We try to go where our customers go. It's really as simple as that."

After MTV included *The Hills* within vMTV, Pepsi signed on to be a sponsor, creating a "category-exclusive, branded-content program" that included Pepsi vending machines that dispensed virtual product with virtual coins. Pepsi products went on to be the top-selling product in 2007 with more than 110,000 cans being "virtually recycled" and used more than 650,000 times. The study also cited that the cans were observed in use over 2.4 million times by 85% of the user base. "Those are very high numbers," commented Vail, "To have people in-world using their virtual MTV bucks to buy Pepsi at those rates was amazing to us." Armed with the favorable research findings and with more research in the works, it can be assured MTV Networks and Pepsi will be doing more within the cross-section of television and interactive platforms, and that it will impact the new version of vMTV.

While the very nature of virtual worlds is the endless possibilities of a global audience, some iconic brands are perfectly content to focus in on just one or two markets. At the end of 2007, Levi's launched its first virtual world in Hong Kong and China targeted to Internet sophisticated teens and young people aged 15 to 24.

Using the same basic formula of customizable avatars as virtual stand-ins for socializing and public chatting, the clothes on these avatars in Levi's World are limited to just one brand: Levi's. According to press releases, users can "play games, chat with each other, invite their buddies, try to buy the latest Levi's collections, and participate in a host of daily online events including DJ music nights, singles nights and celebrity chats. They can earn and spend virtual money in both the virtual world and in real world stores, where limited edition items can be redeemed."

Although Levi's has been in There.com selling virtual versions of the company's clothing for some time, the company is no stranger to virtual brand experimentation. *The New York Times* reported, back in 1996, how the company worked with NTT Software Corporation (an American subsidiary of Nippon Telegraph and Telephone Corporation) to create online 3D game environments where players/avatars flew over San Francisco Bay in search of targets in an attempt to promote the brand's image as innovative.

Levi's in its Hong Kong/China virtual world venture hopes to "reinforce its unique brand experience by engaging this particular geographic audience and providing ways for youths to connect with each other and to the Levi's brand and jeans collection, ultimately driving members to real world Levi's stores." While at the time of this printing, it's too soon to predict how Levi's Asian foray will go, at least one advertising agency, Leo Burnett, has put in their own two cents via the company's blog stating, "Launching a branded virtual world should have a 'wow' effect, otherwise it might very well damage the brand's image. In this case, the thought sounds better than the reality."

Sources

available from: //www.pbs.org/mediashift/2007/10/digging_deeperyour_guide_to_vi.html

Barbie.com, available from: http://www.nytimes.com/2008/05/08/technology/personaltech/08basics.html?_r=1&ref=personaltech

Disney, available from: http://news.softpedia.com/news/Cartoon-Network-039-s-FusionFall-Delayed-Again-for-Further-Polishing-83630.

shtml; http://venturebeat.com/2007/08/01/disney-buys-club-penguin-in-700-million-deal/; http://nextup.wordpress.com/2008/05/05/does-disney-get- virtual worlds/

Kids users, available from: http://www.virtualworldsnews.com/2008/04/virtual world-2.html

Levi's, available from: http://query.nytimes.com/gst/fullpage.html?res=9A0DE4D81E39F937A35750C0A960958260

Levi's in Hong Kong, available from: http://www.imediaconnection.com/news/17092.asp

Mattel, available from: http://www.virtualworldsnews.com/2007/08/barbiegirlscom-.html

Michael Pole, NBA quote, available from: http://metaversed.com/tags/news/ new-worlds

MTV, available from: http://www.virtualworldsnews.com/2008/02/interview-gamin.html; http://www.worldsinmotion.biz/2008/05/report_brandings_ influence_on.php

Neopets, available from: http://www.forbes.com/prnewswire/feeds/prnewswire/2008/02/14/prnewswire200802141358PR_NEWS_USPR_NYTH110.html

Pepsi & MTV, available from: http://www.adweek.com/aw/content_display/news/agency/e3i26f1bfd408799a204314aa22cf15c8a5?pn=1

Ravi Mehta/MTV, available from: http://virtualgoodsinsider.com/2008/04/ 28/virtual-goods-branding-101/

Sony, available from: http://en.wikipedia.org/wiki/PlayStation_Home

5

SUCCESS STORIES

success |sək'ses|

noun

1. the accomplishment of an aim or purpose

■ the attainment of popularity or profit

"If you're serious about success in the virtual world, you should be thinking about how you can build relationships with – and earn the loyalty of – the community you hope to engage. Focus on the value you can provide in order to entice residents to voluntarily spend time with your brand."—*Nancy Baym, Blogger*

"Successful virtual worlds encourage creativity, imagination, and fun."—*Joey Seiler, editor of* Virtual World News *reported to the BBC*

WHAT'S THE MEASURE OF SUCCESS?

Success – everyone wants to attain it, but few know how. Success is a term that is bantered about loftily from the press to boardrooms, but within the realm of branding what does success really mean? Is success quantifiable by metrics, or is it simply, as the actual definition states, accomplishing a specific purpose?

In the branding world, there is and always has been much debate on how to define the success of a brand campaign of any sort – from building a new identity from scratch to social networking events. After 15 years in the business, I have personally yet to be won over by a means to accurately track ROI for branding efforts or by people who put too-much-faith in metrics as a measurement of success. Branding is and always will be one part science, one part creativity, and one part pure psychology. Measuring the potential for success of a new name intended for a tech product in more than one national market will almost always fall flat in test groups even it does very well once out in the marketplace.

Within virtual worlds, measuring success via traffic metrics tells about as much of the actual success story as it does within the mainstream 2D web – in essence not too much. Blogger Nick Wilson rants, "With the proliferation of AJAX based web applications which bork the whole concept of a 'page view,' the rise of social networks and blogs where brand control is a laughable concept and, the widgetization of the web, where content becomes untethered and free, *traffic as a measurement of success is ridiculous*" [Emphasis added]. To Wilson's point, traffic becomes all the more inane as a virtual world measurement. As we know, overall traffic numbers vary within the worlds, and given that many brand-oriented campaigns are more event-driven within virtual worlds, traffic in and of itself doesn't account for how and to what degree people actually engage with the brand. So what if 10,000 people visited Avnet's Museum in Second Life in a given week? Did they walk away with positive thoughts and associations of Avnet based on their experience, or did they fly away thinking how ridiculous the display is? (And no, I'm not trying to bash Avnet here – it's simply an example of possible outcomes.) Without some means of exit interviews to provide qualitative information about a brand experience, no one would ever know the measurement of success based on this example. It's also an interesting point that worlds like There.com and Second Life are not isolated from the rest of the Internet – meaning that brand campaigns may indeed take place in-world, but there is also a lot of activity that goes on within the rest of the Internet and particularly social media activities like blogging, Facebook, Twitter, etc. as both promotion of an in-world event/campaign and discussion by the people of it. Therefore, looking at success metrics of Second Life alone isn't the whole picture.

If 100,000 people pick up free virtual goods from brands like Nissan, Herman Miller and Dell in-world, is the measurement of success based on how many people pick-up the freebies and then go to buy an actual car, office furniture piece or computer? Hopefully, you're vigorously shaking your head "of course not." In an ideal world, the virtual consumer would become a real one. But perhaps a better and much more realistic measure of success is how many people you are actually reaching with your overall or specific campaign message. As we saw from Pepsi and vMTV's research studies in the previous chapter, how are you changing people's perceptions of your brand based on the experience of engaging with it? How many people in the US walked away from Pontiac's Motorati Island with a virtual Pontiac thinking more highly of Pontiac's edginess (versus stodginess)? Again does traffic alone fill in these blanks? No, but the point is, success is really in the eye of the beholder based on what the original intent/goal was. If it was achieved – woohoo! If not, go on to the next chapter on failures.

EXAMPLES OF CO-BRANDING IN VIRTUAL WORLDS

An example of success is Coke's contest to develop vending machines to be distributed within Second Life. In the summer of 2007, Mike Donnelly, Director of Global Interactive Marketing for Coca-Cola professed a thing or two about the success of the campaign jointly developed with C.C. Chapman and Steve Coulson of Crayon to the 2007 Second Life Community Convention.

Like many major brands, Coke was already in Second Life before the actual company ever was – being designed by Second Lifers with unofficial "counterfeit" vending machines and Coke products. After the creation of the Coke Virtual Thirst Pavilion by virtual world agency Millions of Us, the relationship between Crayon and Coke led to a contest for Second Life residents to design an imaginative yet usable vending machine to be placed in various locations within Second Life. If you're pondering why on earth avatars would have a need for drinking a Coke to quench their thirst in-world, you are probably missing the point of virtual worlds that anything can be created – including very real world actions. The end results of the winning entry by Second Lifer Emerie May (a.k.a. Ann Marie Mathis) showed plenty of spunk and imagination including arctic wildlife snowglobes, a wild bubble ride and "magic Coke bottles" presented as a giant puzzle, which when solved, dispensed the desired Coke product (see Screenshot 5A). Ann Marie's winner's statement was, "The essence of my idea is this: have the bottle be a vehicle to the experience. Make it immersive and cool, and then give me something to take away that adds to my everyday Second Life experience. I wanted something that residents will like and use."

To its credit, Coca-Cola (fueled by its past experiences with its own virtual world, in-world presences in Habbo and World of Warcraft, and guided by Crayon and Millions of Us) presented the contest/campaign as one about "dispensing experiences" versus product (see Screenshot 5B). Does the number of Coke bottles the machines dispense ultimately define the

SCREENSHOT 5A   Coke Virtual Thirst Contest in Second Life

success of the campaign? If you ask *Wired* writer Frank Rose, the answer is a resounding "yes" based on his major focus on Coke in his July 2007 article for *Wired* titled *How Madison Avenue Is Wasting Millions on a Deserted Second Life.* (Yes, it's safe to say the article was not in favor of Coke's efforts.) But for Mike Donnelly, the answer is "no." The definition of success is based upon the internal criteria the company set. Donnelly told the 2007 convention that the media doesn't always get what defines success within virtual worlds. "I feel like I've been used as the sacrificial lamb," stated Donnelly, "We wouldn't be spending the money in SL if we agreed with the [Frank Rose] *Wired* article."

Donnelly went on to say that social media was tracked and measured surrounding the contest/campaign with an emphasis on branding (engagement and message) versus marketing

SCREENSHOT 5B   Coke Virtual Thirst Contest in Second Life

(to sell more Coke) to measure success. The resulting metrics he cited were:

- 300 blog posts on the contest/campaign;
- 33,000 links;
- 150+ photos in Flicker.

For Donnelly and his team, the experience Coke gained were lessons learned, and by the definition of their own initial goals, success.

More on Coke's Virtual Thirst Lessons Learned

At the 2007 Second Life Community Convention, Mike Donnelly, Director of Global Interactive Marketing for Coca-Cola cited lessons learned from the experience and advice to other major brands looking for success in-world:

1. Listen to the community. Do not talk at customers.
2. Partner with pros.
3. It's about community, not location.
4. Embrace your critics and learn from them.
5. Maximize success, use multiple channels.
6. Strike a balance between art and science.

Another Kind of All-American Past Time

By now, most non-virtual world users have at least heard mention of the XXX-rated places to go, people to see – and well other things to do – within Second Life in particular. Creative sex pose balls and upper and lower body parts to customize an avatar with (for sale of course) are just a couple highlights of the sex business alive and kicking within SL. On that basis, it may be no surprise then that legendary men's magazine *Playboy* is equally at home in SL. But what is surprising is Playboy's PG-13 approach to SL in order to purposely head off tawdry comparisons via the press. Playboy's island is *all* about the brand including the shape made to resemble its infamous Playboy bunny's ears, with the left ear completely covered in the full black and white Playboy logo that is in actuality a pool. The foray into Second Life is reported to have begun as a means to promote Playboy online store (playboy.com) with live (in-world and sometimes real world streamed into virtual world) comedic and music events.

Dancing, music and hang-out spots abound on Playboy Island, but you'll find nary a sex pose ball nor "all nudity, all the time." The brand was actually criticized by users and diehard fans for not making the pool the social focal point of the island and for purposely nixing a virtual Heff mansion – all of which

SCREENSHOT 5C   Playboy

were done in an effort to keep the brand's SL presence PG-13. In fact, the most flesh one will see is Euro-style topless sunbathing and pool lounging (see Screenshot 5C.)

What is also interesting about the Playboy SL model is how it treats its in-world retail boutique, complete with Bunny branded bikinis, hoodies and the infamous Hugh Heffner smoking jacket. Marc Girolimetti, founder of Green Grotto Studios and the man responsible for bringing Playboy into Second Life told Aliza Sherman a.k.a. Cybergrrl Oh on her SL Business show, "We really treat this like a real retail location. We set pricing, we see what works and take things off sale. We do apply real world business methodologies to run this place. It's not a crap shoot by any stretch of the imagination. We do our own analysis to see what products work and don't work. Some things are taken off line and some are taken off line to give away during events we have." Boxers are L10 (Linden dollars) and the Heff smoking jacket a pricier L25. Originally conceived to use virtual versions of real-life retail products to drive the sales of those products online, Playboy's strategy has since been altered to create more products exclusive to Second Life and without real world counterparts. Why the change in strategy? Sales simply weren't as high as expected.

Another feature of the island is Cherries Jazz Club, offering "set" details such as a concert grand piano, guitar, harp, and bar with details like the Playboy bunny logo wrought in bamboo. Since Playboy did not want to run the Sim themselves, they handed over the tightly reigned brand to its community of users for the opportunity to create the brand experience. Instead of allowing millions of SL people do whatever/whenever, a crew of "employees who understand SL more than most" were created to work there on a weekly basis. The Playboy Bunnies do abound here, but not everyone can be a Playboy Bunny – they have to be hired as a part of the crew. As of Winter 2008, there was a 100-person waitlist to become one. Success, it seems, is in Playboy's court.

WHAT COMPANIES CAN LEARN FROM "GRASS-ROOT" VIRTUAL BRANDS

Both Coke and Playboy have used *co-branding* successfully in virtual worlds mainly by co-mingling their brands with others to create major events such as "Rock The Rabbit" where Playboy commissioned iconic music acts such as Iggy Pop and Duran Duran as well as newcomer bands to design their own Playboy t-shirts which are then available in-world, online and at real world Bloomingdales.

Playboy, however, isn't limiting their co-branding to big names – KO Designs, Alpha Male, Sharkture, Simply Spoiled are just a few grass-root, SL fashion brands created by individual resident designers that have been commissioned by the company in-world. These brands are considered the top tier of virtual fashion designers within Second Life and were asked to create exclusive SL-only Playboy collections to be offered within the Playboy store. Playboy is also giving the designers a rather rare opportunity to re-sell portions of their own clothing line in the in-world boutique to expand their brand. The move was initially received extremely well from residents and bloggers.

In the same vein, L'Oreal Paris launched different virtual make-up looks to apply to an avatar (including "Vintage Glamour" featuring actress Penelope Cruz and "Some Like It Scarlett" featuring actress Scarlett Johansson) by avoiding the L'Oreal island and co-branding with in-world store brands such as Love, Aly, Calla, Minx, Nuclear Boutique and Nicky Ree to promote, stock and distribute the free make-up looks (see Screenshot 5D). Advertisements for the looks as well as the stores appear in SL magazines and websites devoted to virtual fashion and clothing. (Like the real world, the number of virtual fashionistas is quite high and a phenomenon in and of itself.) The strategies were touted as "one of the first examples of a real world major brand promoting a virtual world partnership strategy."

Wagner James Au, author of *The Making of Second Life: Notes from the New World* and former Linden Lab employee told blogger Jerry Weinstein that the best thing marketers can do to key in on success in-world is to create "a targeted campaign that really leverages what SL is and what it's best at – dynamic collaborative creation and freeform fun. The brands that have stayed have made more of an effort to engage the community, and have a consistent presence."

To do so, of course, takes real work and real commitment both in time and money. It is interesting at this juncture of virtual world development to hear just how many companies are putting a tepid toe in the waters for shorter and shorter

SCREENSHOT 5D   L'Oreal Paris Campaign

periods of time before pulling out. The place for short-term campaigns aside, if the major purpose for showcasing a brand in-world is for branding (image/message) versus marketing (for actual sales), not being willing to remain in-world and readjust strategies as needed is really just as illogical as the infamous "build it and they will come" model of both the early dotcoms and early brands in virtual worlds. Bigger brands can take a lesson from successful virtual world entrepreneurs (the kind who are making profits and an actual living) with the willingness to devote time and creative resources just as is required in the real world. As Daniel Terdiman, author of *The Entrepreneur's Guide to Second Life: Making Money in the Metaverse* puts it, there aren't any "shortcuts to success for virtual entrepreneurs," ditto for large brands.

Sources

Coke, available from: http://www.virtualworldsnews.com/2007/08/coke-comes-clea.html

Daniel Terdiman, available from: http://www.wired.com/techbiz/people/news/2007/11/terdiman?currentPage=1

Loreal, available from: http://www.kzero.co.uk/blog/?p=1614

Nancy Baym, available from: http://www.onlinefandom.com/archives/community-brand-success-on-second-life/

Nick Wilson, available from: http://metaversed.com/14-may-2007/traffic-useless-measurement-success-virtual worlds

Playboy, available from: http://www.slcn.tv/real-biz-sl-playboy; http://nwn.blogs.com/nwn/2008/03/smart-bunny-pla.html

Wagner, J.A. (2008) *The Making of Second Life: Notes from the New World*, New York: Harper Collins.

6

FAILURE STORIES

failure |ˈfālyər|

noun

1 lack of success

2 the omission of expected or required action

3 the action or state of not functioning

■ a lack or deficiency of a desirable quality: *a failure of imagination.*

"No matter. Try again. Fail again. Fail better." *—Samuel Beckett*

FAILURE DEFINED

If you asked most journalists in 2007 if virtual worlds and Second Life in particular were the next great thing in technology and culture, most would have responded with a fervent "yes" – at least judging from the quantity of article buzz that year (including my own for *Brandchannel.com*). By the end of 2007, however, the tides turned and suddenly Second Life could do nothing right in the eyes of many including the press. Many of the same major publications who breathlessly gushed about virtual worlds earlier in 2007 began a bashing campaign – blaming companies for spending too much, virtual agencies for doing too little (perhaps other than cashing checks) and SLers for just being SLers. Yes, a lot of companies spent a lot of money. (And for the record, very few will actually fess up to just how much.) Yes, many, many mistakes were made. And yes, there were and always will be some legitimate failures – not because these companies tried but mostly because they *ceased* trying.

Just as we defined success in the last chapter as accomplishing intended goals and objectives, failure is the lack of accomplishment and the cessation to continue.

WHAT WENT WRONG

As I've gathered information for this book, I've been taken aback at just how many professionals are quick to bash Second Life in particular dubbing it a virtual wasteland for advertisers/marketers, and how quickly everyone involved is so terribly disappointed and disillusioned. While I personally believe some of these can-do-nothing-right stories are written for the same reasons the original walk-on-water ones were (to sell publications), I don't see it as all bad. After all, isn't the whole point of virtual worlds a chance to experiment with experiencing and interacting within a 3D Internet? Aren't mistakes going to be made to learn from? Rather than regarding virtual worlds as another medium through which to distribute a message, with the highly distinct added bonus of interacting more than usual with customers and potential customers, it seems there have been, and perhaps still are to a certain extent, many people who proclaimed virtual worlds the holy grail of new branding.

If you ask Gartner, consultancy and research firm, virtual worlds are full to the brim with failures. Gartner cites that an astounding "Nine out of ten business forays into virtual worlds fail within 18 months but their impact on organizations could be as big as that of the Internet." The focus on technology rather than "user requirements" is one of the prime failure factors according to Gartner.

LESSONS LEARNED

"Businesses have learned some hard lessons," said Steve Prentice, vice president and fellow at Gartner. "They need to realize that virtual worlds mark the transition from web pages to *web places* [emphasis added] and a successful virtual presence starts with people, not physics. Realistic graphics and physical behavior count for little unless the presence is valued by and engaging to a large audience."

Steve Prentice, in my view, is right on the money with refocusing expectations of virtual worlds. I particularly like what he states about seeing static web pages as transitioning to "web places" by virtue of the advent of virtual worlds. Having consulted many companies on branding during the dotcom hey day, it's hard to believe that so many managers and executives still fall for the technology versus people hook when looking at new, important technology movements and for the "hey, they're doing it, so we better get on it!" mentality to take over, despite the fact that the company probably doesn't get what "it" actually is. It's another fantastic example of what has been described as "following the technology" rather than looking at the culture of users within the technology, and how the technology can help reach actual human beings with very real human behaviors and attitudes.

The other great downfall leading to failures is not having specific objectives (remembering our definition of success in the previous chapter) based on specific target audiences.

While Habbo Hotel and Club Penguin may have much more specific audiences than There.com or Second Life, the burden is still on each business and their agency partners to be as clear and specific as possible about who exactly they're trying to reach, keeping in mind that personas, actions and behaviors tend to be bolder and more exaggerated than real-life or even 2D Internet ones. Adds Steve Prentice, "The challenge that generic projects inside Second Life face is that they do not know who their audience is and therefore do not know what their needs are. Organizations cannot effectively market a product for the whole world."

Despite the harsh numbers, Gartner still expects that by 2012, 70% of businesses/organizations will establish their own exclusive virtual world to be used at the very least for internal corporate purposes, citing greater success due to "lower expectations, clearer objectives and better constraints."

In mid 2007, Proximity Worldwide, a global interactive and direct marketing agency, publicly stated seven steps that they believe lead to failure of brands online:

1. Playing 'LogoCop' with your brand.
2. Being dull, boring or useless.
3. Behaving exactly as you do offline.
4. Hiding the truth.
5. Believing there is a difference between human needs online and offline.
6. Confusing 'peer to peer' with 'targeting'.
7. Assuming you have a right to be there.

Of Proximity's seven steps, two through six are dead on.

If you don't believe it, take a look at these numbers. That same year Komjuniti, a Hamburg-based research firm, polled 200 Second Life residents of which 72% were disappointed with real world company activities in Second Life and just over 40% considered these efforts a one-off not likely to last.

"The most successful business people in Second Life have taken a look at the commercial landscape and determined where needs exist," Catherine Smith, Linden Lab's director of marketing told *Brandweek* in 2007. "If you are not authentic and do not offer anything to the community, you are likely to be ignored."

Ben & Jerry's and Splenda are a couple of consumer brand examples within Second Life that severely flopped with residents. Both featured as very cartoonish perhaps more apt for a 3-year old than a sophisticated Internet user. "Splenda sucked wind," lamented Aliza Sherman, Web 2.0 consultant, writer and SL Business show host, "They really could have engaged residents who are looking for mindless fun – not a bad thing – but they built and abandoned."

Indeed the build and abandon approach to virtual worlds is partly what put the fly in the ointment for many journalists (not to mention residents) looking for the tantalizing tidbits other journalists were extolling earlier. More often than not, a "presence" is built within the worlds with little to see, little to do and in some cases absolutely no one "manning the booth." Can you imagine a consumer company building a large retail location and leaving it empty save from a few product samples and branded signs? It would never happen in the real world. Yet, so many companies were and are taking this approach with virtual worlds, wondering why they're not getting very far.

On the other end of the failure scale is simply not going far enough. While Jean-Paul Gaultier (see Chapter 3) took the less-traveled path of using Second Life as a temporary, event-driven forum, more companies have sought both successfully and not-so-much to have a ongoing presence within virtual worlds, and frankly, have not been so shy to use every gimmick and (in particular) contest in the book in-world. Geek Squad, those lovable, nerdy computer tech support guys and girls, proudly displays its sci-fi best via Geek Squad's Volcano Island – complete with volcano, futuristic survival shelter and blinding, radioactive orange at every turn. Mimicking its real world retail presence, US-based electronics store Best Buy, the island has an avatar on site dressed in the Geek Squad requisite white button-up shirt, pocket protector and black pants uniform to answer any of your technical including SL questions.

While there are some whimsical, interactive features to the island, it's an example of a company that doesn't go far enough with the in-world features, therefore creating huge missed opportunities. As of the middle of 2008, desks, computers, phones and even branded product boxes are displayed to resemble a real-life store environment, yet no actual services can be placed in-world nor is lead generation possible. An interactive quiz is offered to see if one is "ready to be a real Geek" by working at the store, yet no recruiting is actually done out of SL nor are any HR web links provided. To make matters worse, some features are highly difficult to use such as the lifts and pods to explore the museum and futuristic views of Geek Squad, thereby sending a mixed branding message of "we exist to make your life technically easier" yet you *may* actually need to be a rocket scientist to explore our island fully. It's a minor but clear case of poorly thought-out details getting in the way of the brand and its message.

As Second Life garners an ever-longer list of business branded sites that are virtually deserted, virtual worlds in China are having very similar experiences. Across the seas, three competitors to Second Life in China have set up shop: HiPiHi, NovoKing and UOneNet – the latter of which are still in Beta testing in mid-2008 to very small audiences and the first of which went live in Spring 2008 to mass audiences.

HiPiHi is the eldest of the trio of China-based virtual worlds as well as the largest with a reported 48,000 registered users. But so far, the Second Life-mimicking virtual world is yielding many of the same results as the American one it's trying to emulate: not many people are showing up. Global brands such as P&G, Intel, and Hewlett-Packard have created presences within HiPiHi such as floating billboards and a virtual Vidal Sassoon salon (called "VS Midnight Salon") to target a mostly male 20-something audience. Although senior external relations manager at P&G, Heidi Wang told *Businessweek* in May 2008 that, "We see HiPiHi as more of a platform to reach a young and trendy generation, to provide them with a brand new online experience, and as a signal to the general public that VS is leading the trend," thus far the self proclaimed trend setters are yielding empty salon results.

Habbo, one of the largest virtual worlds and social networking services for teens in the rest of the world, also failed miserably in China closing its doors altogether in August 2007 after only one year in existence. *Virtual World News* reported that "The challenging Chinese market and high operational costs led to the decision of closing the service." While pricing models and lack of Shockwave technology among Chinese users were also speculated as reasons for closure, the most interesting fodder in the rumor mill was that Habbo, from its simplistic graphic renderings to its game model, did not fit the Chinese culture. Period, what has been so wildly successful in many other countries was put into play cookie-cutter style within the Chinese market – without much regard for the cultural differences in users.

What is uniquely different to virtual worlds versus the rest of the Net is the ability for users to *create* their own environment, community and experience. And if you don't think that users are creative types, you clearly haven't spent much time in a virtual world. Aside from the fact that many virtual world adult users are the "creative class" either professionally, semi-professionally or by interest, teens and younger are simply natural born creative types. Research firm, Pew Internet reported in 2008 that 64% of teens aged 12 to 17 create their own content online (up from 57% in 2007).

It's my view that the major path to failure (in addition to the points cited earlier) is ample amounts of *business arrogance*. Arrogance comes out as:

1. Assuming the "right" to be in-world.
2. Creating buildings, billboards and other empty vessels full of branded signs and messages yet devoid of any life or personality.
3. Creating copy-cat contests, promotions and theme park-like activities that are lacking originality and spark.
4. Assuming that businesses and agencies "know better" (or are more creative) than the actual users.
5. Forgetting that users are target audiences, critics and co-creators in real time.

In regard to point four, it is the other way around in many cases, which is most evident by looking at the in-world success of grass-roots brands such as within the Second Life fashion industry. What businesses have thus far failed to understand is that the majority of virtual world users are not adverse to brands in-world. What they are adverse to are stale, arrogant, lifeless brand efforts that either discount users all together and/or discount their own creativity. Virtual world residents want to play and interact with a brand in a fun, refreshing, and meaningful way. The absolutely last thing they want is to be sold to, and the absolute, absolute last thing they want is to be subjected to a lot of brand hype with no or faulty delivery.

No matter how you cut it, failure by brands in virtual worlds is failure to engage with imagination and creativity and failure to change.

Sources

Chinese Virtual Worlds, available from: http://www.virtualworldsnews. com/2007/06/brands-need-to-.html; http://www.jackmyers.com/ commentary/virtual-world-report/17196341.html; http://www.wired. com/gaming/virtualworlds/news/2007/08/virtual_bank; http://www. businessweek.com/technology/content/may2008/tc2008055_089117. htm

Gartner, available from: http://www.gartner.com/it/page.jsp?id=670507

Habbo Hotel China, available from: http://www.virtualworldsnews.com/ 2007/08/habbo-hotel-chi.html

Linden Labs, available from: http://www.brandweek.com/bw/news/recent_ display. jsp?vnu_content_id=1003563242

Proximity: http://www.virtualworldsnews.com/2007/06/brands-need-to- .html; http://www.jackmyers.com/commentary/virtual-world-report/ 17196 341.html; http://www.wired.com/gaming/virtualworlds/news/ 2007/08/virtual_bank

7

NEW CHALLENGES

"Behind the rosy predictions of virtual reality . . . lie concrete challenges for computer graphics, distributed systems, security, human-computer interaction, and social science."—*The Virtual Worlds Group, Stanford Computer Science Department*

VIRTUAL WORLD STANDARDS (THE CASE OF IBM)

As most people know by now, virtual worlds are fraught with technological glitches and challenges. A highly limited number of SIMS (i.e., users and their virtual "stuff") can be in any one place at any one time without the system becoming incredibly slow or crashing all together; creating and navigating avatars is a slow, clunky process that severely tests patience and is far from natural; and despite the fastest high-speed Internet connections mainstream users have ever enjoyed, worlds can be very slow to work with. Multimedia streams (including Flash technology) that are commonly seen elsewhere on the Net are not available to use seamlessly within virtual worlds, and there is currently no portability between worlds or between the worlds and the web. In other words, my avatar in Second Life and all the virtual goodies she possesses are confined to the "walls" within Second Life and cannot be the same in There.com or any other virtual world. It's also interesting to note that the vast majority of virtual worlds are Windows-based only, entirely ignoring users of Mac, Linux, Red Hat, etc.

Within the halls of corporations around the world, other challenges are emerging: from hacker prone, unsecured areas and lack of firewalls (with the exception of IBM as noted in Chapter 3) to new, HR challenges of hiring avatars in-world (such as greeters) to represent the company. The Internal Revenue Service, otherwise known as the US Tax Agency, declared in 2008 that in-world greeters are officially employees hired by a company versus an independent contractor and must be taxed as such. As Dave Elchoness, a labor and employment law attorney and HR consultant, commented to BNET, "An employment relationship with a greeter in Second Life is almost more complicated than the relationship with a regular employee who might go online any time someone enters the company's virtual offices. You may be hiring someone . . . you don't know anything about." Knowing nothing about a potential or newly-hired employee in-world is a more-than-likely reality given that virtual worlds are built around real world anonymity – which doesn't do much to help internal branding efforts. Further, lawyers familiar with virtual worlds state that there are "no in-world mechanisms for enforcing employment agreements. If an avatar or a virtual design firm does not show up for work, there is little the hiring company can do if no formal contract exists in the real world."

Because behaviors by avatars both from "civilian" residents and business employees in-world can be wilder and more exaggerated than in real life, some businesses are left wondering as to what is and what isn't acceptable protocol in-world. IBM has handled this situation for its currently 6000 employees with avatars in-world by developing comprehensive guidelines called "Guiding Employees in the Metaverse." Although the guidelines are not exactly the same as employee codes of conduct in the real world, they are reflective of the company's business conduct guidelines and address specific topics such as avatar appearance, behavior, and intellectual property protection. IBM also prevents its employees from conducting company business in public spaces in-world unless requested to do so by a customer. Corporate espionage is indeed live and well within virtual worlds. (And if you're skeptical about that claim, it's interesting to note that the real world espionage concerns are large enough to motivate the Central Intelligence Agency in the US to create a few virtual islands for internal use such as such as training and unclassified meetings, according to the *Washington Post*. Google Earth has also been criticized by special interest groups and governments as presenting not only an invasion of privacy at the individual level but a potential threat to national security. In the Fall of 2007, *The Guardian* reported that the al-Aqsa Martyrs' Brigades used Google Earth as a tool to plan Qassam rocket attacks on Israel. A number of similar terrorist concerns have been reported around the world.)

As one of the first large organizations to create employee blogging guidelines in 2004 and "Netizen" guidelines in the mid-1990s, the IBM virtual world guidelines were put together by IBM's Virtual Universe Community which the company describes as "a growing internal organization to which IBMers exploring virtual worlds can contribute as we refine these guidelines and deal with new challenges as they emerge." The guidelines are made available on the Internet to the public and cover 11 topics summarized, by permission, here:

IBM Virtual World Guidelines: Summary

1. **Engage:** IBM encourages its employees to explore responsibly – indeed, to further the development of – new spaces of relationship building, learning and collaboration.

2. **Use your good judgment:** As in physical communities, good and bad will be found in virtual worlds. You will need to exercise good judgment as to how to react in these situations – including whether to opt out or proceed.

3. **Protect your – and IBM's – good name:** At this point in time, assume that activities in virtual worlds and/or the 3D Internet are public – much as is participation in public chat rooms or blogs. Be mindful that your actions may be visible for a long time. If you conduct business for IBM in a virtual world or if you are or may appear to be speaking for or on behalf of IBM, make sure you are explicitly authorized to do so by your management.

4. **Protect others' privacy:** It is inappropriate to disclose or use IBM's or our clients' confidential or proprietary information – or any personal information of any other person or company (including their real name) – within a virtual world.

5. **Make the right impression:** Your avatar's appearance should be reasonable and fitting for the activities in which you engage (especially if conducting IBM business). If you are engaged in a virtual world primarily for IBM business purposes, we strongly encourage you to identify your avatar as affiliated with IBM. If you are engaged primarily for personal uses, consider using a different avatar.

6. **Protect IBM's and others' intellectual property:** IBM has a long-established policy of respecting the intellectual property of others, and of protecting its own intellectual property. Just as we take care in our physical-world activities to avoid infringement of intellectual property rights and to provide proper attribution of such rights, so we must in our activities in virtual worlds – in particular with regard to the creation of rich content.

7. **IBM business should be conducted in virtual environments only with authorization:** You should not make

commitments or engage in activities on behalf of IBM unless you are explicitly authorized to do so and have management approval and delegations. If you are authorized, you may be asked by IBM management to conduct IBM business through a separate avatar or persona reserved for business use. You should certainly decide to use a separate avatar or persona if you think your use of an existing one might compromise your ability to represent IBM appropriately.

8. **Be truthful and consistent:** Building a reputation of trust within a virtual world represents a commitment to be truthful and accountable with fellow digital citizens. You may be violating such trust by dramatically altering your digital persona's behavior or abandoning your digital persona to another operator who changes its behavior. If you are the original creator or launcher of a digital persona, you have a higher level of responsibility for its behavior.

9. **Dealing with inappropriate behavior:** IBM strives to create a workplace that is free from discrimination or harassment, and the company takes steps to remedy any problems. However, IBM cannot control and is not responsible for the activity inside virtual worlds. If you are in a virtual environment in conjunction with your work at IBM and you encounter behavior that would not be acceptable inside IBM, you should "walk away" or even sign out of the virtual world. You should report abuse to the service provider. And as always, if you encounter an inappropriate situation in a virtual world which you believe to be work-related, you should bring this to the attention of IBM, either through your manager or through an IBM internal appeal channel.

10. **Be a good 3D Netizen:** IBMers should be thoughtful, collaborative and innovative in their participation in

virtual world communities – including in deliberations over behavioral/social norms and rules of thumb.

11. **Live our values and follow IBM's Business Conduct Guidelines:** As a general rule, your private life is your own. You must, however, be sensitive to avoid activities in a virtual world that reflect negatively on IBM. Therefore, you must follow and be guided by IBM's values and Business Conduct Guidelines in virtual worlds just as in the physical world, including by complying with the Agreement Regarding Confidentiality and Intellectual Property that you signed when you became an IBM employee. It is obviously most important to do so whenever you identify yourself as an IBMer and engage in any discussions or activities that relate to IBM or its business, or use any of IBM's communications systems or other assets to participate in a virtual world.

INTELLECTUAL PROPERTY THEFT

IBM's number 6 on the list of protecting its and others' intellectual property is indeed a tall order and the subject of enormous amounts of controversy within virtual worlds in general. Imitation is said to be the best form of flattery, but for real people and companies who worked diligently to create something unique, imitation is just a crime, period. Virtual worlds have opened up a huge Pandora's Box on intellectual property issues because it is so easy to copy someone else's work without agreement from the originator thanks to open-source programming. The problem manifests in many ways but a few of the most distinct ways are design and trademark infringement committed against grass-roots entrepreneurs and design and trademark infringement committed against well-established brands. Call it the "Clone Wars" of virtual worlds.

Kevin Alderman, founder of Eros LLC, a company that sells Second Life avatars with realistic genitalia and sex actions, filed suit in 2007 against an avatar named "Volkov Catteneo" for pirating his SexGen Platinum product, which sells for US$45. After contacting Linden Lab prior to the suit to resolve the pirating, Alderman's Abuse Reports and DMCA (Digital Millennium Copyright Act) complaints were ignored. "We begged them, please do something about this," Alderman told *Popular Science's* webzine.

According to Reuters, Alderman and his attorney filed an "Eros LLC vs John Doe," case with the US District Court in Tampa, Florida that accuses the Catteneo avatar (who's identity is not known in real life) of illicitly copying and selling a SexGen product for far less than what Eros sells it for, therefore undercutting Eros' sales.

The intellectual property case filed against a "John Doe" where the real world identity is not known is a precedented legal practice for cases involving the Internet. Record labels are perhaps the best-known cases of this strategy when they attempted to sue thousands of anonymous people for illegal music downloads, copies and sharing. In Alderman's case, his attorney attempted to subpoena chat histories and financial records from both Linden Lab and Paypal to establish the avatar's true identity.

Although Linden Lab provides detailed instructions on how to file a complaint under the Digital Millennium Copyright Act (DMCA) so that copyright-holders may seek legal remedy if their online designs are copied, virtual worlds were something lawmakers who passed the act in 1998 never foresaw.

Sean Kane, a lawyer specializing in virtual worlds told Reuters, "The reason the DMCA was enacted was for companies like AOL. I don't think courts will look at [DMCA] and say Linden Lab is an Internet service provider."

Although some people may not have much sympathy for folks in the adult sex businesses, Alderman's problems and lawsuits are all-too-real for many entrepreneurs and artists across industries – and even celebrities.

On the "uncensored" version of SL Exchange available in Second Life as well as via the 2D Internet, celebrities down to their most private body parts (including tattoos) are cloned for any virtual resident to buy and present as his or her self. Body doubles of Demi Moore, Little Kim, Angelina Jolie, Iman, Sharon Stone, Reese Witherspoon, Pamela Anderson and even Gillian Anderson of the X-Files fame are just a small sample of who are available for L$500 with skin and hair sold separately. The products are marketed with the celebrity's name and photo along with the virtual rendition of them for purchase. Do these celebrities have grounds to protest? Yes, but clearly not many are aware that their own celebrity brand is being violated.

In worlds that are based on user creation, some users seem to feel a certain entitlement to anything and everything that can be created graphically. Some people do it for the fun of it; others are motivated by the profit of it. The problem is so prevalent that a legal non-profit organization set up shop in Second Life called Virtual Intellectual Property Organization (VIPO), which offers "accessible legal advice concerning virtual property, trade and commerce and the use of real-life intellectual property in virtual worlds" to especially support artistic and scientific endeavors. VIPO was started and run by American intellectual property attorney, Tamiko Franklin. According to Franklin, VIPO specifically offers "consultations on outside world intellectual property protection as well as management of virtual property in-world. We have assisted resident authors in structuring license agreements, drafting "cease and desist" notes, even protecting musical works and works of visual art while also providing information regarding related rights."

Of course along with protection and management come enforcement measures and resolutions of disputes. While there is no official court system in place (an attempt at Second Life Superior Court failed miserably in 2005), a loosely based English common law system is underway including a High Court through Metaverse Republic. Fines and ultimately banishment would be the in-world penalties for lost cases.

DIGITAL DOMAIN LAW

Real world courts struggle to define and keep up with virtual world happenings as they apply to real world laws country by country. The *Washington Post* reported that Japanese authorities arrested a man in 2005, for allegedly committing "virtual muggings" within MMORPG Lineage II through software that assaulted and robbed game avatars and after would sell the stolen virtual items for actual money.

In the same Washington Post article, Philip Rosedale, the founder and former chief executive of Linden Lab, stated that "Second Life activities should be governed by real-life laws for the time being." Rosedale walked his talk but calling in the Federal Bureau of Investigations (FBI) on more than one occasion for reasons including checking whether Second Life's virtual casinos complied with US law – to which the answer was "no." Gambling has since been banned on Second Life (as is online banking and investment due to several SL banking scandals).

HIJACKED BRANDS

If the brand is high profile enough, it will likely show up in-world in some form or fashion regardless of whether the company is in-world or not as noted by Coke prior to entering Second Life with their Virtual Thirst campaign. The current Linden Lab policy is to investigate Abuse Reports filed as a complaint regarding trademark infringement and if found in violation, remove the products. The unfortunate part is that the company is reported to not actively search for trademark violators, which, like the real world, leaves the burden squarely on the brand police.

Benjamin Duranske, founder of the Second Life Bar Association and an actual lawyer, told Reuters in 2007 that trademark infringement occurred in at least 1% of Second Life transactions – equaling approximately 1.4 million per year. A search within Second Life turns up in some cases hundreds of "fake" luxury brands cloned in-world to be sold at a profit. Gucci, Rolex, even Nike are, like in the real world, crowd favorites. However, these companies don't authorize repro-duction of their products for virtual ones. Brand counterfeit-ing is a difficult enough problem to monitor and deal with in the real world. Put the same scenario in a virtual world and a brand is literally hijacked.

A company who refuses to have some sort of official pres-ence – whether as an actual store or to sanction "authorized resellers" – is literally giving away its brand to people who will do whatever they want with it commercially and actually make some money doing it. The head-in-the-sand strategy made famous by many luxury brands with their reluctance to officially be on the web for many years is (to say the least) highly ineffective and ultimately costly to the brand.

Herman Miller, the iconic furniture designer and maker (see Screenshot 7A), is one brand to fight back against counterfeits in-world and out. Herman Miller took its real world campaign called "Get Real" and applied it to Second Life with the help of River Runs Red at the end of 2007 by doing an amnesty pro-gram of sorts for knock-off buyers. It offered its 15 piece

SCREENSHOT 7A   Herman Miller Get Real Campaign
Source: River Runs Red

collection for L$300–L$850 (approximately US$1.40 to US$3.50) for virtual decorators. However, users who bought knock-offs previously received the authentic HM collection for free in exchange for deleting the knock-off items in their possession as a time-limited, honor-based offer. An interesting approach to a common problem – but Herman Miller couldn't avoid the real world task of "cease and desist" letters to several in-world counterfeiters. The results, it seems, are mixed.

Sources

Celebrity clones, available from: http://uncensored.slexchange.com/modules.php?name=Marketplace&MerchantID=10061&page=2
CIA, available from: http://www.washingtonpost.com/wp-dyn/content/article/2008/02/05/AR2008020503144_pf.html
Google Earth, available from: http://en.wikipedia.org/wiki/Google_Earth#National_security_and_privacy_issues

Herman Miller, available from: http://virtuallyblind.com/2007/10/ 08/herman-miller-second-life/; http://news.cnet.com/8301-13772_3-9794128-52.html

HR/IBM/BNET, available from: http://findarticles.com/p/articles/mi_ m3495/is_11_52/ai_n21130490

IBM, available from: http://domino.research.ibm.com/comm/research_ projects.nsf/pages/virtualworlds.IBMVirtualWorldGuidelines.html

Kevin Alderman/DMCA, available from: http://www.popsci.com/ category/tags/kevin-alderman

Metaverse Republic, available from: http://www.metaverserepublic.org/ building-our-constitution/executive-summary/

Reuters, available from: http://secondlife.reuters.com/stories/2007/05/ 29/protecting-real-brand-names-in-a-virtualworld/

Stanford, available from: http://vw.stanford.edu/

VIPO, available from: http://virtuallyblind.com/2008/01/27/vipo-second-life/

Washington Post, available from: http://www.washingtonpost.com/ wp-dyn/content/article/2007/06/01/AR2007060102671.html

8

THE FUTURIST'S REVIEW

future |ˈfyoō ch ər|
noun
1 (usu. **the future**) the time or a period of time following the moment of speaking or writing; time
regarded as still to come:

■ events that will or are likely to happen in the time
to come:
■ **a prospect of success or happiness.**

future life
noun
*a future state or existence, especially seen as very different
from the present*

**"The future will be better tomorrow." —Dan Quayle,
Former Vice President of the United States**

REFLECTIONS ON STRATEGIES AND TRENDS

From the time I first began this book with my friends at
Palgrave-Macmillan to as you read this book, the landscape of
virtual worlds has changed – a lot. As a consultant and writer,

it has been an interesting and frankly head spinning arc to watch in such a short amount of time. And because of the rapidity of change, it makes me realize why bigger brands are struggling to break in or keep up. The phrase "Come on, old man [brand] – keep up!" comes readily to mind with the 10-year-old sprinting ahead by leaps and bounds of the (in his own mind) youthful 45-year-old.

In today's landscape, it's true that by the time a campaign can feasibly be planned and executed within a virtual world, the strategies could be obsolete or at the least old hat. And if you aren't listening to the reflections and ideas of younger generations as a part of a brand's team or at the very least overall strategy, yes, I'm sorry to tell you, you're doomed. It's a young person's Internet (even with Baby Boomers aspiring to be young) and scaling younger with new generations being born to iPods and web-enabled cell phones as a given in life. The trends and new adoptions start with them. Listen up – you might learn something more valuable than a 35-year-old creative director can tell you.

"If you snooze, you lose." *—A nine-year-old kid*

IMPACT ON BUSINESS AND BRAND STRATEGIES

Blink your eyes, and it's over. Don't think for a moment you have a handle on virtual world branding just because you completed this book or read a few other articles on it. Twenty-first century technology is full of *rapid, real-time changes* that are only accelerating, and that my dear friends is the most significant challenge to both writing a book on the subject and to branding successfully within virtual worlds. Things change so quickly in the virtual world environment – be it technology, trends or tastes – that not keeping apace with fresh thinking guarantees strangulation of a brand within these mediums. In the virtual world environment – and I would argue Web 2.0 frontiers in general – lack of monitoring what's going on out there and a resistance to participate equals far too many missed opportunities:

> "Virtual worlds are important in the same way that the Web was important in the early- and mid-1990s but nobody could yet figure out how or why. That is where virtual worlds are at this moment – but unless we allow companies to throw money at them, we'll never make any progress in learning more about why we all should be there in the first place. Ultimately, vws are venues for community, connection and communication – ingredients for a great marketing tool." —*Aliza Sherman, Web 2.0 Consultant, CybergrrlOh in Second Life*

You may say, well if it's that much trouble, why bother? Is it really worth investing in? I remember quite vividly attending Internet conferences in the early 1990s with executives asking the same thing about what we now take for granted as ordinary websites. So in case you're still wondering, the answer is "yes." Why? Because the grand experiments being done in virtual worlds matters to the future of the web. The lessons you can learn with these new mediums matter in regard to making your brand a tangible and valuable experience *as it relates to your brand message and objectives*. Like it or not, interactively experiencing the web beyond a two-dimensional web page is the future of the Internet, and the amount of users ready to adopt new habits are only growing – and growing up:

> "We've grown up believing that what most of us want to do for entertainment is passively consume things – that the way to have fun is to sit back and absorb something where it has no interaction whatsoever . . . Technology

has for the last fifty years only allowed us to deliver experiences of the sort where we had to sit and just listen to them. —Philip Rosedale, founder & former CEO of Linden Lab

Directly dialoguing and interacting with perhaps not all but some of your existing customers, past customers, potential customers, and lest I forget, influencers on your customers are all critical factors in the future of the Internet, especially within social media. Younger audiences are beginning to expect it. The days of blasting a point-of-view via a one-way mirror (be it the television, brochure, print ad or news story) are becoming obsolete because a brand's narrative through advertising and marketing is rapidly being usurped by two- or multiple-way conversations and interactions. Beyond marketing, concept, prototype, product and service testing with virtual focus groups will be used even more to develop and validate ideas and concepts. McKinsey & Company, the management consultancy have recently been quoted as saying that companies "absolutely" must be "experimenting in virtual worlds" to get the attention of anyone under the age of 30. And no, you're not imagining it, a bit of Attention Deficit Disorder is required to keep up with it all:

> **"People like to interact with other people. People like to interact with their environment in more visceral ways. It's the way our brains work." *—Irving Wladawsky-Berger, Chairman Emeritus, IBM Academy of Technology***

> **"We live in a 3D world, our brains are organized in three dimensions, we might as well compute in three dimensions." *—Ray Kurzweil, Inventor, Futurist***

Faster, more powerful computers and faster Internet connections are needed and will happen to tip the point over to mass acceptance by making these virtual worlds, especially 3D ones, less cumbersome and easier to use for mainstream users (and of course, the younger the users are, the faster they're going to learn how to navigate these worlds anyway). Cell phones with more converged technologies and greater capabilities will make mobile accessing of virtual worlds viable and easy and will create more opportunities for mobile-only virtual worlds and/or brand extensions of existing, successful worlds. As of Spring 2008, this is already occurring with Vollee's client that puts Second Life on web-enabled phones. Moore's Law, the 40-something-year-old prediction made by Intel co-founder Gordon E. Moore that the number of transistors on a (silicon) chip will double approximately every 2 years, will continue (Intel says until the year 2022) – bringing faster computing, more capabilities and decreased associated costs, with the next movement, predicts inventor/futurist Ray Kurzweil, as 3D computing:

> **"You can imagine mixing virtual worlds with reality augmentation, to bring elements of the real world into the virtual world, and elements of the virtual world into real-life, with people, avatars, buildings, rooms and furniture that are only virtually present, but appear to be real (until you try to touch them)." —Mitch Wagner, Executive Editor InformationWeek.com**

The "walls" of the existing virtual worlds will start to fade and borders between worlds will blur as portability takes shape whereby a user of Second Life or other virtual world can walk into another world with the same avatar and possessions with the same ease as simply visiting another website. An MTV concert sponsored by BMW, live from Munich's Olympia Halle features a virtual VIP backstage meet and greet for fans around the world and live press conference for international news agencies with headlining bands, while BMW prototype cars are presented to a lucky few as virtual give aways – all of which can be accessed from multiple worlds – not just the host one. Future Wikia puts this melting of boundaries as between 2010 and 2015. There.com has already introduced an instant messaging client, called ThereIM, allowing users to text and chat between the 3D virtual world and 2D world as has Second Life with its Slim which also features voicemail for offline friends. Social networking news site *Mashable* stated: "Allowing communication between the virtual world and the regular online world is a major hurdle that has hampered wider acceptance of that platform. Taking down this barrier will be a boon not only for entertainment purposes but also for commercial and corporate endeavors. Enabling interaction between these two separate worlds will surely take 3D virtual worlds to the next level."

As of July 2008, Linden Lab and IBM successfully demonstrated virtual world interoperability by teleporting avatars between the Second Life Preview Grid and an OpenSim virtual world server. Important for enterprise and the future of netizens alike, "Interoperability is a key component of the 3D Internet and an important step in enabling individuals and organizations to take advantage of virtual worlds for commerce, collaboration, education, operations and other business applications," stated Colin Parris, Vice President, Digital Convergence, IBM:

"The ultimate dream is to merge the real world and the virtual world into a totally seamless experience."
—*Photosynth Project, Microsoft Live Labs*

In addition, the boundaries between "real life" via photos, videos, video chat, satellite photos and 3D graphic renderings blur and merge, enabling users to visit real-life cities with their actual tourist destinations and businesses as a virtual explorer. Notre Dame, quaint local café in the eighth arrondissement and

Chanel Boutique on rue du Faubourg St Honoré, anyone? Following my earlier example, what about a virtual tour of Kaufingerstrasse in Munich (home to many large department stores and chains) during the BMW-sponsored concert intermission? The possibilities and combinations thereof are limited only to imagination and ingenuity. Google Earth and EveryScape (see the Virtual World Companion Guide) are already going in this direction. As of June 2008, Disney announced its massive Walt Disney World in Orlando, Florida is accessible to tourists via Google Earth where it has taken 100,000 shots from eight photographers to build 1,500 3D images of Disney World structures. Virtual world users are *hungry* for things to do. Faster computing, according to Intel, will also mean real-time translations from one language to another, such as an English speaker hearing a French speaker in English (and vice versa) via real-time translations. And yes, these capabilities are already being played with by a handful of companies.

The technology of virtual reality "touch" is not as far off as you might imagine. Researchers at Queen's University in Belfast are developing technology that will bring the sense of touch to virtual worlds. The field of "haptic technology" will allow a future where shoppers can feel the products they want to buy online, or get a sense of force when the ball hits the racquet in a digital tennis game. (This is already seen in Nintendo's Wii video game system.)

Researchers are reported to be spending the next 3 years working on the network architecture to support haptic technology that isn't delayed through network connections.

Professor Alan Marshall, project leader, explains that "the stereoscopic images used to create 3D worlds are actually ideal for haptic technology, because they create the dimension of depth essential to touch – which has exciting implications for adding another of the real human five senses to virtual environments."

"Media companies are smarting after letting independent Internet companies such as Google and Facebook get ahead of them with web search and social networking, so they are loath to fall behind again with virtual worlds. Even if today's Second Life doesn't satisfy the mass market, dozens of other virtual worlds will spring up tailored to each personal taste along the Long Tail of niche content online." —*Mark Glaser, Journalist & New Media Critic*

Virtual world competition will heat up and there will be many virtual worlds available versus the one singular metaverse first imagined by Neil Stephenson and colleagues. Just as there are many 2D website destinations, there will be choice and variety in worlds with easier access between them. How specific the target of each world remains is an interesting debate. If things continue along the successful trends of virtual worlds for kids, tweens and teens based on well-known brands and entertainment tie-ins, the possibilities for even more targeted worlds are exponentially larger than that existing today – such as for Baby Boomers who love to cook. The next major age group focused on will undoubtedly be babies/toddlers based on the rise of digital/electronic gadgets and toys (such as VTech and Leap Frog products) as well as "baby smartening" videos and software sales and consumer interest:

"Nortel Networks is looking to the next generation of employees to shape the workplace of tomorrow, and high on its agenda is exploring the role of Web 2.0 technologies and virtual worlds such as Linden Lab's Second Life." —*Natasha Lomas, ZDNet.co.uk*

"One of the venture capitalists I spoke to said that 95 per cent of the business plans he sees at the moment seem to have virtual worlds in them." —*Michael Parsons, Editor of CNET.co.uk – from the Virtual Worlds Forum 2007*

New generations of workers who feel comfortable and confident with new technologies will work virtually from all parts of the globe (including rural areas) as if they're all working out of the same room. While larger corporations may leave established worlds like Second Life because of IT security risks, identity fraud and privacy/ confidentiality concerns, in-company training, meetings, collaboration, etc. will migrate to their own private virtual worlds – in all likelihood on the same technological platforms created by just a few tech companies.

General Manager of IBM Lotus software Mike Rhodin's, number one prediction is, "The Virtual Workplace will become the rule. No need to leave the office. Just bring it along. Desk phones and desktop computers will gradually disappear, replaced by mobile devices, including laptops that take on traditional office capabilities. Social networking tools and virtual world meeting experiences will simulate the feeling of being there in-person. Work models will be changed by expanded globalization and green business initiatives that reduce travel and encourage work at home."

> **"The definition of 'meetings' will radically transform and become increasingly ad hoc and instantaneous based on context and need. 3D virtual world and gaming technologies will significantly influence online corporate meeting experiences to deliver more life-like experiences demanded by the next generation workers who will operate more efficiently in this familiar environment."**
> **—Mike Rhodin**

Meetings and personal interactions will be further enhanced by life-like human gestures such as Linden Lab's "Lip Sync" feature using a PC's microphone to mimic lip motions. VR Wear is one company taking the personal gestures further by connecting to the user's webcam to record and analyze gestures such as smiling and nodding yes and no and then reproducing them exactly on the avatar in Second Life.

The virtual worlds with active in-world economies will ebb and flow just like the real world ones. Second Life saw a sharp downturn in in-world spending when gambling was banned, but did anyone consider virtual real-estate sales hit a similar "land bubble" to cause lower sales? Just as in the real world, economic conditions in-world will influence spending. Therefore, adjust brand strategies accordingly. On the plus side, if discretionary spending becomes tighter and tighter based on the current economic downturn in at least the US market, spending the equivalent of US$1.38 on a virtual bauble may actually rise in frequency because it's viewed as an "affordable" luxury. Or perhaps will the same happen as in the 2003 recession?

"I can't tell you how many people I met then who were out-of-work programmers and web designers creating content in SL while they looked for jobs." —*Wagner James Au, Second Life Blogger & Author*

With these predictions said, will they stand up to the fluctuating landscape over the next couple of years?

"The most exciting thing about new applications going forward will be the surprises I cannot predict. The most important things are usually the ones that people within the industry do not see. They tend to develop outside the industry. I do not know. I just wait to be surprised with the next one that comes along." —*Gordon E. Moore, Intel Co-Founder*

Maybe, maybe not – they're educated guesses based on recent clues. But foreseeing the future and "getting it all right" is really not what branding is about. As a brand professional and technology lover, there are a few things I've learned to expect in the new age of branding: Expect to be surprised. Expect the unexpected. Expect to respond to change quickly. Expect that someone will have a better idea. All the same, give it your best in branding a new world. No one said innovation was easy, but it sure is worth it.

Sources

Disney World/Google Earth, available from: http://origin.mercurynews. com/google/ci_9499355

FutureWikia/Photo Synth, available from: http://future.wikia.com/wiki/ Virtual_Reality

IBM/Linden Lab Interoperability, available from: http://www-03.ibm.com/ press/us/en/pressrelease/24589.wss

Irving Wladawsky-Berger: http://www.usatoday.com/printedition/money/ 20070205/secondlife_cover.art.htm

Mashable, available from: http://mashable.com/2008/09/04/secondlife-slim/McKinsey & Company, available from: http://technology.timesonline. co.uk/tol/news/tech_and_web/article3803056.ece

Mike Rhodin IBM Prediction, available from: http://eightbar.co.uk/2008/ 03/ 25/ibm-virtual-worlds-1q-2008-roundup/

Mitch Wagner, available from: http://www.informationweek.com/blog/ main/ archives/2007/09/the_future_of_v_1.html

Moore's Law/Gordon Moore, available from: http://www.intel.com/ technology/mooreslaw/index.htm

Nortel/ZDNet, available from: http://news.zdnet.co.uk/communications/ 0,1000000085,39292545,00.htm

Philip Rosedale, available from: http://www.youtube.com/watch?v=BbY_zA Ot-Ug

Ray Kurzweil, available from: http://www.businessweek.com/globalbiz/ content/may2008/gb20080519_782410.htm?chan=globalbiz_europe +index+page_top+stories

Touch/Haptic Technology, available from: http://www.worldsinmotion. biz/2007/07/29-week/

Vollee/Second Life on Mobile Phones, available from: www.blog.newsweek. com/blogs/levelup/archive/2008/04/21/second-life-on-your-mobile-phone-yes-says-vollee.aspx

Wagner James Au, available from: http://nwn.blogs.com/nwn/2008/04/ subprime-mortga.html

VIRTUAL WORLD COMPANION GUIDE

At the time of writing this book, I was actually surprised to find that there is no one, comprehensive place to find information about all the different virtual worlds in the marketplace despite the wealth of partial listings online. Hence, the birth of the *Brand Avatar Virtual World Companion Guide* created to give you a brief snapshot/overview of the many worlds in the marketplace. The following is meant to be a companion guide to introduce you to the various virtual worlds grouped by target audience and type of virtual world and subsequently listed in alphabetical order. Although several worlds have multiple target audiences (such as There.com for 13-year-olds through to people in their 20s), many have a single target audience (such as Habbo for teens only).

The *Brand Avatar Virtual World Companion Guide* categorizes vws into "only" sections (such as kids only, teen only, etc.) as well as by vw type/style. With monsters to kill, quests to complete and treasures to win, classic MMORPGs are some of the stickiest on the web with millions of hours logged online per month. However, for purposes of this companion guide, only a few that incorporate other virtual world characteristics (social networking and/or economy) are listed in detail below. An additional list of classic-styled MMORPGs is listed by name only.

You'll notice that some vws have been around since the middle of the 1990s while others are being pixeled out as fast as a venture capital company can mint them and are in Beta testing as of this writing. Because virtual world environments and business models change so quickly, this printed guide is not meant to be 100% inclusive of all worlds, 100% accuracy cannot be guaranteed and descriptions may have changed since yesterday. The online version of this guide can be found at: http://www.demesabrands.com/brandavatar.

The *Brand Avatar Virtual World Companion* could not have been completed without the kind help of Betsy Book, creator of the Virtual Worlds Review website, run from 2003 to 2006. Some descriptions from Virtual Worlds Review are included in the guide below. Massively.com and KZero also served as valuable online sources while the rest was compiled either directly from the world or by third-party sources on the Internet.

VIRTUAL WORLDS FOR GENERAL AUDIENCES

3B Rooms

http://www.3b.net
Windows only
Launch Date: Late 2006
Target Audience: kids and older (minimum ages not specified)
Revenue Model: advertising

3B Rooms is a cross between a 3D virtual chat room and a web browser. Using the free software you can visit or create your own customizable avatar and 3D rooms whose walls are lined with websites to click through to visit. Visiting and shopping on websites such as Gap Men, Amazon.com, and eBay while text chatting with other avatars is among its unique features. Over 200 retail stores are reported to be a part of the site. On their own site: 3B's online social experience enables users to hang out and chat in customizable 3D spaces called villages. These are spaces built to display their own: MySpace pages; friends' pages; favorite websites; Flickr photos; and more.

In addition to creating a personalized avatar, which they can dress and design, the user can personalize their village by choosing a 3D theme for their space and changing some of the elements inside the village.

Examples of 3D themes available for the village include art gallery, auto, beach, girly, the lounge, New York, party, prom, retro cafe, sky lounge, soccer, spa, techno, hiphop, weddings, football and basketball.

Active Worlds

http://www.activeworlds.com
Windows Only
Launch Date: Public Launch 1997
Target Audience: 18-year-olds and up
Revenue Model: premium subscription, advertising, platform customization

Active Worlds first went Beta in 1995. Since then the company has changed management several times and is currently operated by Activeworlds Inc. Members help develop the world by building objects that visually enhance each world's setting but don't appear to do much else. Unlike the futuristic themes of worlds like Cybertown, Active Worlds is full of modern-day cities with a new age utopian twist. There is a distinct "international" theme, with many worlds based on real world countries.

In addition to maintaining its publicly accessible virtual worlds, Activeworlds Inc. licenses its technology for private development of educational, e-commerce, entertainment, and promotional projects. AWTeen is the teen-only spin-off.

Cybertown

http://www.cybertown.com
Windows Only

Launch Date: 1995
Target Audience: teens through twenties
Revenue Model: premium subscriptions, advertising, sponsorships, product placement

An early Blaxxun project, Cybertown is a virtual world with a futuristic sci-fi theme greatly influenced by the cyberpunk genre of literature and film. Cyber-citizens are encouraged to build homes or purchase a custom designed one, get in-world jobs to earn CityCash and bank at the Town Bank or invest in the Cybertown Stock Exchange, participate in Cybertown's elaborate political system, and become "a respected citizen of a large intergalactic online community." When that gets to be too much, avatars can let off some steam by going clubbing or visiting in-world concerts and movie theaters or simply by playing the CityCash lottery. According to Cybertown's website, other features include: a private 3D VR (virtual reality) home with your own personal chat, inbox, message board and free e-mail; and Cybertown shopping malls and flea markets (it was inevitable with all the 3D stuff available), virtual pets and ongoing role-playing games.

While most virtual worlds recognize the general influence of Neal Stephenson's concept of the "Metaverse" in the novel *Snow Crash*, Cybertown is the closest to attempting to recreate the Metaverse as it is described in the novel, complete with a Black Sun Club for dancing and music.

Cyworld

http://www.cyworld.com
Windows and Mac
Launch Date: 1999, US 2006

Target Audience: 16- to 30-year-olds (Asia), 16- to 24-year-olds (US),
Revenue Model: In world commerce

Cyworld is South Korea's most popular social networking site. A cross between virtual world and MySpace-style profiles, the site experienced phenomenal growth since its acquisition by SK Telecom in 2003. Since then, a US version has been introduced allowing users to create their own profile (dubbed a "Minihome"), their own avatar ("Minime"), and their own space ("Miniroom") to meet new people, stay in touch with friends, send messages, upload photos, exchange gifts, etc. A "Minihompy" (a miniature home page) is one of the most popular features. The site is reported to be the most popular with 20-somethings in Korea where 9 out of 10 people in the 24 to 29 age bracket are members. The target US audience is younger: 16- to 24-year-olds.

The company has expanded over the last couple of years into other countries including China, Taiwan, and Japan. It remains to be seen whether Cyworld's huge success in Asia translates to the US. The company closed its European operations based in Germany in 2008.

Everyscape

http://www.everyscape.com
Windows Only
Launch Date: Beta 2008
Target Audience: 18-year-olds upwards
Revenue Model: Business customizations, commerce planned

EveryScape claims to not be an online world, but rather "the world online." Call it an enhanced map service, the realistic

3D virtual world in Beta as of 2008 takes users from the streets of the world's cities and towns such as San Francisco, Beverly Hills and Bejing to inside the buildings, businesses and sights lining the streets. The unique vw brings businesses, organizations and consumers together to "build and share their world the way they see it." Businesses in particular get the opportunity to create the branded, virtual retail experience just as a consumer would view it in the real world. It is a direct competitor to Google Earth.

Faketown

http://www.faketown.com
Windows and Mac
Launch Date: 2000
Target Audience: 14- to 35-year-olds
Revenue Model: premium membership, in-world currency, advertising

Faketown is a 2D virtual world involving gaming and social networking. Played directly in an Internet browser (no downloads required), users create profiles, build a virtual home, create drawings, upload mp3s and video, and vote in weekly mayoral elections. "Fake IDs," which simply represent players in the game are available as is "fake coin" currency, which can be obtained through the game or by buying it with real world money (US$1.00=100 fake coins). Fake coins also buy items at Faketown auctions and real estate.

Frenzoo

http://www.frenzoo.com
Windows Only
Launch Date: Beta 2008

Target Audience: teens to 20s
Revenue Model: advertising, product placement

Frenzoo is a 3D vw/social networking site based in Hong Kong that capitalizes on virtual world interest in fashion. Frenzoo enables users to connect with friends by becoming "budding fashionistas". Avatars and all the avatar accoutrements including branded clothes, footwear, accessories, furniture, and lifestyle items are customizable.

Frenzoo features a "RealFashion 3D Engine" that realistically simulates a user's character, clothing and living environments. Social network pages and messaging are part of the experience. Frenzoo is reported to be aspiring to "be an ideal advertising network for big brands looking for creative ways to penetrate the teen demographic."

Gaia Online

http://www.gaia.com
Launch Date: 2003
Target Audience: 13-year-olds and upwards with an emphasis on teens
Revenue Model: in-world commerce, site products/special collectibles, gift cards

Founded by "a few comic book fans in a garage," Gaia is an anime-themed virtual world aimed primarily at teens with "imagination and Gaia Gold," the official in-world currency. An "Avatar Arena" where avatars compete based on their looks (an interesting twist on antiquated barbarian practices), chat forums on a myriad of subjects, art contests and of course avatar and space customization are the highlights.

Gaia Cash allows members to buy the more exclusive Gaia store items (that are not readily available for purchase with

Gaia Gold) as well as any regular Gaia store product or monthly collectible instantly. Gaia Cash can be purchased directly from the site, or redeemed from Gaia gift cards available at US cheap chic retailer Target stores or Rite Aid drugstores and/or special promotions. As of the beginning of 2008, Gaia has 3.5 million users.

Google Earth

http://earth.google.com
Windows, Mac, Linux
Launch date: 2005 (re-launch)
Target Audience: Not specified
Revenue Model: premium products

Google Earth is not a classic virtual world where multiple users can interact with one another as avatars, but it earns a spot in the guide because of its use of 3D images to create a 3D, photo realistic virtual interaction and tour of geographic and tourist destinations around the world, including features that allow the user to change camera positions/viewpoints similar to the offerings in Second Life. Google Earth allows users to fly anywhere on Earth and see satellite imagery, maps, terrain, 3D buildings and even explore galaxies in space. When viewing, some buildings/structures can be clicked on to see a summary description about it, such as Coit Tower in San Francisco.
Google Earth 4.3 Features include:

- photo-realistic buildings from cities around the world;
- dawn to dusk views with the Sunlight feature; and
- swoop navigation from outer space to street-level.

The basic product is downloadable and free but premium products are also available to enterprises and businesses.

HiPiHi

http://www.hipihi.com
Windows only
Launch Date: 2008
Target Audience: 18-year-olds and upwards
Revenue Model: Subscription, in-world commerce, brand promotions, sponsorships

Best described as Chinese version of Second Life. Set in Mandarin, residents retain ownership rights to everything they create. HiPiHi offers two different products: HiPiHi World and HiPiHi Home, a private space for users to invite friends.

Kaneva.com

http://www.Kaneva.com
Windows Only
Launch Date: Beta 2007
Target Audience: 18 to 34-year-olds
Revenue Model: in-world currency, in-world commerce, third party customization of Kaneva platform

3D avatar based world with all the usual components of casinos, malls, apartments, dance clubs, etc. Since its Beta launch, Kaneva has been considered by many a "disruptive" technology among virtual worlds due to its marriage of 3D virtual world environments a la Second Life and social networking a la MySpace, YouTube and Facebook. Users go between Kaneva's web browser-based social networking experience and the site's connected 3D virtual world. On the 2D portion, users create their own profiles, join groups, meet others, and interact via messaging, blogs, tags, and media sharing (sharing of photos, videos, music, games, etc.). In the 3D portion, users can create their own 3D avatars, personalize their homes, accessorize their 3D worlds however they seem fit, and meet other people via their avatars. In June 2007, Kaneva was the first virtual world site to integrate synchronized viewing of YouTube videos within their 3D virtual world.

Meet-Me

http://www.meet-me.jp
Windows Only
Launch Date: 2008
Target Audience: children to adults (exact breakdown unknown)
Revenue Model: in-world transactions, advertising

Meet-Me is Japan's kinder, gentler, cleaner and (in general) better mannered answer to Second Life and China's HiPiHi. Avatars are designed rounder and softer, often compared to Pokemon characters (versus the angular and relatively realistic Second Life avatars) and interact in a virtual Tokyo by commuting the typical Japanese way such as riding trains or other vehicles, walking and running. Unlike Second Life, flying and teleporting are not options. Pornography-free and designed to be a safe environment for children as well, Meet-Me offers Japanese users cyberspace shopping, entertainment, games and even Christmas lights. Free to join.

Metaplace

http://www.metaplace.com
Windows and Mac
Launch Date: Closed Alpha 2008
Target Audience: kids and older (not specified further)
Revenue Model: in-world commerce, others unknown

Metaplace's motto is: build anything, play everything, from anywhere. Metaplace is out to change how virtual worlds are created by offering a Do-It-Yourself virtual world platform.

Metaplace dubs itself a next-generation virtual world platform "designed to work the way the web does." Build it worlds, social interaction with profiles and games with badges earned (think Boy Scout merit badges based on game tasks completed), content creation and commerce are among the primary features at this stage. Metaplace-created virtual worlds can be embedded into external sites, including Facebook, MySpace or a blog. Virtual worlds in the Metaplace network can also be easily linked together and found by user profile, rankings and reviews.

Moove

http://www.moove.com
Windows Only
Launch Date: 1997
Target Audience: 14-year-olds and up
Revenue Model: premium subscription

Moove is a 3D virtual world that offers multilingual versions of its product called "Roomancer." Roomancer is a play on words that reflects the room-building focus of Moove as well as the "romance" angle of the world. Indeed, Moove's home page highlights room-building and online romantic encounters as the primary activities available to visitors.

Moove's avatars are called "actors" (perhaps another play on words with "moove/movie"?) and the choices range from human avatars to animals and robots. While the default selection of body types is minimal, there are many outfits to choose from in Moove's online store and it is relatively easy to establish a virtual home in Moove. New visitors are given their own collection of rooms and are encouraged to begin immediately decorating their online home with a selection of furniture. Each member hosts and manages his/her own space, which allows a great variety of individual expression.

Virtual Worlds Review stated that the average age of Moove visitors is higher than most virtual worlds, and it is not uncommon to see ages in the 40s, 50s, and even 60s in Moove profiles. Currently offered in several languages, the company is German based.

Openlife Grid

http://www.openlifegrid.com
Windows Only
Launch Date: Beta 2007
Target Audience: 18-year-olds upwards
Revenue Model: unknown

Openlife Grid is an Australian-based, 3D world built with open source technology from the OpenSimulator project to create a global community. It positions itself as a promising new alternative grid to Second Life. According to Sakai Openlife (Real Life name: Steve Sima) the founder, "Openlife is moving towards a 'provider' path where ISPs and Web Hosts would also be able to provide resources. So as a user or company, having your own presence or land in-world could be purchased from many providers, reducing the cost and keeping it affordable for all." The world as of this printing is not fully functioning and does not have an in-world currency.

Rocketon

http://www.rocketon.com
Windows and Mac

Launch Date: Closed Alpha 2008
Target Audience: 15-year-olds upwards
Revenue Model: unknown

RocketOn is a San Francisco based start-up that's making a 2D virtual world that users can access across any site through an embeddable widget that enables chat with other avatars. Users can chat in real time with other people on the network and walk into a variety of themed worlds (chat rooms) with different features. Still in closed alpha phase as of the time of this writing, the company states it's working on a web-based virtual world that "transcends the single site approach and creates a parallel, avatar-based experience on almost every website available." Gaming á la MMORPGs is also reported to be a part of the offering.

Red Light Center

http://www.redlightcenter.com
Windows Only
Launch Date: 2006
Target Audience: 18-year-olds upwards
Revenue Model: premium membership, advertising affiliates, sponsorships, brand placement, in-world commerce, banner and billboard spaces, in-world events

Yes, you knew someone had to do it. Red Light Center is an all-sex, all-the-time virtual world based out of Nevada (perhaps best known as the state for legal gambling and brothels in the US). The 3D virtual red light district based on the real one in Amsterdam offers customizable avatars, fantasy profiles with the ability to upload erotic photos, plenty of places for "sex," and real world sex products and toys through its in-world store. Community events, art openings, and dancing are available for those in-between moments. Entrance to the world and socially hanging-out is free, but getting intimate with fellow "networkers" costs. Needless to say, no minors are allowed.

Second Life

http://www.secondlife.com
Windows and Mac
Launch Date: 2003
Target Audience: 18-year-olds upwards
Revenue Model: premium subscription, in-world currency and commerce, advertising, sponsorships, product placement

Second Life is a highly imaginative, creative environment built exclusively by residents. *Virtual Worlds Review* likened a visit to Second Life to "stepping into a Dali or Magritte painting in 3D." The "fully textured high-resolution" avatars are customizable to the "nth" degree, with dozens of sliders to change every micro-pixel of your avatar's shape, size, and color. While some "Lifers" (the preferred nickname of Second Life citizens) do their best to create miniature versions of their offline bodies, many use the opportunity to make themselves look as strange as possible. You never know what (or who) you'll see in Second Life, which is part of the appeal.

Although many gamers visit Second Life, it is not a "gaming" world per se. The main in-world activity is the building of interactive objects using a scripting language that is theoretically designed to be simple enough for those with no previous programming experience. This fits in with Second Life's stated goal of encouraging widespread group participation and creativity. Objects can be either donated to the world or can be sold for "Linden Dollars."

Second Life's often bizarre "waking dream" atmosphere may appeal more to creative artist and techie folks than to the casual social chatter. The world is so rich in features, that there is a bit of a learning curve to overcome to get started, which is somewhat alleviated by well-written help files available at the site and a first-visit tutorial. The very name "Second Life" conveys the idea that this is more of a rich, complex online experience than a place to drop by every once in a while for a quick game of "Tringo" with some buddies. If you get freaked out by seeing odd things that you can't explain, this world is not for you. But postmodern surrealists will love Second Life's ever-changing landscape with its stunning scenery and interesting creations. Plus, you can fly!

There

http://www.there.com
Windows Only
Launch Date: Public Launch 2003
Target Audience: 13- to 34-year-olds
Revenue Model: premium subscription, advertising partnerships, in-world currency and commerce

Positioning itself as an "everyday getaway", There has several exotic virtual locales for visitors to explore, including a tropical island setting for virtual surfers, the Goth island Tyr and a simulated Egypt complete with Sphinx and pyramids. Catering for people aged 13 and up, There has "PG-13" standards and is a very social world, with chatting and making friends as the main focus. Members are encouraged to explore There with buggies and "hoverboards" that carry avatars safely and swiftly around virtual terrain.

All avatars are human and can be customized to have a wide-variety of face and body shapes. A favorite activity of There members is the outfitting of their avatars with custom-made clothing items, which can be purchased with in-world currency called "Therebucks." Therebucks can be purchased with a credit card or earned by creating and selling original clothing designs, vehicles and other objects.

Buggy races, hoverboard races, in-world quests and avatar paintball are popular activities and, with the addition of neighborhoods, many Thereians are finding a patch of virtual land to call home.

Traveler

http://www.digitalspace.com/traveler/
Windows Only
Launch Date: 1994
Target Audience: not specified
Revenue Model: unknown

Originally called "Onlive! Traveler," the Traveler technology has been adopted for the greater good by The Digital Space Commons and carefully maintained by a network of Traveler devotees. The ideal world for those who would rather speak than type, Traveler offers a virtual world with built-in real-time voice chat. Not only does this reduce strain on arms and hands, for some it also provides a more emotionally connected experience to the virtual world.

Much like The Palace, there is no central Traveler world but rather a network of user-generated Traveler rooms and worlds with a wide variety of themes. A visitor's avatar in Traveler is a large, expressive head whose mouth moves to mimic the voices of its host. Unfortunately there is no text balloon or chat window alternative for those who prefer not to use the voice feature but communication can take place with other visitors through individual text messaging.

Twinity

http://www.twinity.com
Windows Only
Launch Date: Beta 2008
Target Audience: 16-year-olds upwards
Revenue Model: in-world currency sales, real estate sales, premium accounts

Twinity is a new-to-the-block virtual "mirror" world based in Germany and is described "as a mashup of virtual and real life." "Mirror worlds" are based on a location in the real world, such as a virtual London or New York – or in this case Berlin. Along with the usual avatar (the human species only), space and stuff customization as well as social hangouts and hanging out, "Twinizens" can sell and buy in a real cash economy but do not enjoy as much creative freedom as Second Life citizens. The platform is based on both proprietary and open source systems. An interesting note is that Twinizens must seek approval before selling items due to heightened concerns about copyright infringement.

Virtual Ibiza

http://www.virtualibiza.com
Windows and Mac
Launch Date: 2002
Target Audience: not specified
Revenue Model: advertising, sponsorships

Virtual Ibiza takes online dating service features, blends them with virtual world technology and delivers the result as a trendy social hangout. Thematically based on a real Mediterranean resort island off the east coast of Spain, this world is for visitors ages 18 and older only. Virtual Ibiza's launch press release defines its goal as the recreation of "an online community for those people who love the Ibiza lifestyle." Specifically, this means the 18 to 35 international clubbing community. Virtual Ibiza's avatars appear to take the partying theme to heart as most hold virtual drinks while lounging at various beach, cafe, or night-club settings.

This world is loaded with complementary features for its members, including email, instant messaging, games, message boards, mobile ringtones, and a searchable dating profile area for sharing personal photos and videos. While this is certainly an impressive array of options, the down side is that the inclusion of so many extras tends to divert the focus away from the virtual world itself, which ends up reading more like a subsidiary add-on to the dating profile area rather than the other way around.

The party-club-resort theme successfully gives the space a fun, upbeat energy. But like any party culture, this virtual world seems transitory, like a virtual vacation spot you'd visit every once in a while to hook up but not necessarily a place you'd really want to settle down long term. Still, it's an interesting experiment that attempts to bring the look, feel, and culture of a real world tourist spot into a virtual space.

Vzones

http://www.vzones.com
Windows and Mac
Launch Date: 1995
Target Audience: 13-year-olds and up
Revenue Model: premium subscription, gift certificates

Originally called WorldsAway, VZones is the latest incarnation of a virtual world whose roots go all the way back to the very first visual virtual world, LucasFilm's Habitat (launched in 1985 for Commodore 64 machines). VZones maintains the original Dreamscape world developed by Fujitsu, plus two other worlds called newHorizone and Second Kingdom that must be accessed and paid for separately.

The VZones worlds are colorful 2D environments made up of screen after screen of artistically rendered backdrops. Avatars can be customized with a variety of human body types. More creativity is allotted to the heads, which are interchangeable and infamously prone to being stolen and pawned by head thieves (a problem that can easily be avoided by putting your extra heads in your "pocket"). The three VZones offerings are quite different to appeal to different tastes:

Dreamscape: Getaway environments like beaches, underwater exploration, shopping malls, and casinos make up this world.

newHorizone: A collection of urban environments that are virtual versions of cities like London and New York, this world is home to younger VZones residents.

Second Kingdom: A fantasy-themed virtual world with a combination of traditional roleplay of RPGs and the social aspects of a chat space.

WeeWorld

http://www.weemee.com
Windows and Mac
Launch Date: 2008
Target Audience: 13- to 30-year-olds
Revenue Model: advertising, sponsorships, in-world commerce

Appealing to teens and young adults, WeeWorld is a combination of social networking and virtual world, offering user homepages that are similar to MySpace or Facebook and in addition feature the user's cartoon-based avatar ("WeeMee") that can follow the user on many other messaging and social network sites. WeeWorld offers a personal room for each avatar, which can be decorated and customized by the user as well as a variety of places to chat with other users (as well as interact through forums and messaging) and play games. The company claims "WeeMees get around" with WeeMees available as digital visual identities on the major social and chat networks, in email signatures and blogs. WeeMees are created both in-world and through partner sites such as AIM, Windows Live Messenger, and Skype.

Worlds.com

http://www.worlds.com
Windows Only
Launch Date: 1994
Target Audience: Not specified
Revenue Model: third-party platform customization, future models unknown

During the 1990s Worlds.com built 3D virtual worlds for bands like Aerosmith and brands like IBM, Visa, and Coca-Cola. Site visitors created avatars with customized clothing and also designed their own environments. The company works in partnership with brands for specific market segments to offer multi-user environments with interactive avatars, rich media graphics, text chat, voice-to-voice chat, video and e-commerce. Although not currently active as a vw to the public, the company and its technologies are reported to be restructuring as of 2008.

Zwinky

http://www.zwinky.com
Windows Only
Launch Date: 2006
Target Audience: 13-year-olds upwards
Revenue Model: advertising, in-world currency and commerce,
gift cards, affiliate program

Zwinky is a mash-up virtual world offering "Zwinkies" which
are customizable avatars that are also a part of the MyWeb
Searchbar available on computers running Windows. (MyWeb
Searchbar is available for Internet Explorer, Mozilla Firefox,
Microsoft Outlook, Outlook Express, AOL Email and Browser,
Becky!, IncrediMail, MSN Dial-up Service, AOL Instant
Messenger, Google Talk, ICQ, MSN Messenger, Yahoo!
Messenger, and Windows Live Messenger.)

Users create a 2D avatar to represent him or herself in any
blog or social networking site that supports Zwinkies and only
need to edit the Zwinky's appearance once to update all sites
currently displaying the user's avatar.

In 2007, the next phase of Zwinky or "Zwinktopia" was
launched. Zwinkies could purchase in-world dormrooms
to live in and buy items with Zbucks, the in-world currency,
or a Zcard, the Zwinky debit card. Zbucks are earned by
visiting areas and playing games within Zwinktopia, and by
inviting friends to create their own Zwinkies. Zbucks can also
be added to Zcards using PayPal or a major credit card.

Other worlds targeted to overlapping/general audiences:

Gogofrog

http://www.gogofrog.com

RipLounge

http://www.riplounge.com

VastPark

http://www.vastpark.com

Weblo

http://www.weblo.com

PROPRIETARY BRAND VIRTUAL WORLDS

Barbie Girls

http://www.barbiegirls.com
Windows and Mac
Launch Date: 2007
Target Audience: 6- to 16-year-olds
Revenue Model: retail product, in-world commerce, promotional

Barbie Girls allows users to customize Barbie dolls, dress them up, create virtual homes, adopt pets and chat with other users. The service is free to play with a revenue model focused on the purchase of virtual goods. Barbie Girls is a world filled with parks, cafes and malls to chat with friends and exchange gifts. Girls have two chat options: "B" chat for talking to anyone within the world and "Secret B" chat for friends only.

Barbie girls has taken great care to ensure language is clean and offers a list of acceptable words rather than a list of unacceptable words that are allowed to be used. Members are directed to the Barbie website consistently during their time in the virtual world, and Mattel toys (that appear in the virtual world) are marketed to kids in real life.

Be-Bratz.com

http://be-bratz.com
Windows and Mac
Launch Date: Beta 2008
Target Audience: 6- to 12-year olds
Revenue Model: retail product, promotional, links to on-line commerce, in-world commerce

A MySpace/Facebook-style profile page, mini-games and plenty of in-world shopping. Users purchase a real world Be-Bratz doll, and then use the glam necklace USB key included with the purchase to register in-world.

Coke Studios

http://www.mycoke.com
Windows and Mac
Launch Date: 2002
Target Audience: teens to young adults
Revenue Model: promotional

Coke Studios, part of the Coke Music site at Mycoke.com, is a promotional virtual world targeted to teens and young adults. Members can create their own customized music mixes in a virtual-music studio, play them for other members, and receive ratings for each mix. Favorable ratings allow members to earn points called "decibels" which can be used to purchase virtual furnishings for their personalized studio areas. Members can also earn decibels by participating in a variety of promotional quizzes, games, and contests for Coca-Cola and its partners.

Avatars in Coke Studios are called "V-egos" and can be customized in a variety of outfits. Your V-ego can hang out in one of the many public rooms based on international cities like London, New York, and Moscow or socialize in customized private studios. Coke Studios also offers an in-world messenger feature, which allows communication with other V-egos no matter where you are in the Coke Studios world.

Disney Toontown

http://play.toontown.com
Windows and Mac
Launch Date: 2003
Target Audience: 7-year-olds upwards
Revenue Model: monthly subscription

It's worth noting that Toontown was the first MMORPG project created with children as young as age 7 in mind. This brightly colored cartoon environment offers kids (and their parents) the chance to play games, outfit their toon avatars, own a toon house, and battle the "Evil Cog Robots" trying to take over Toontown and turn it into a bland, black and white, skyscraper-filled, fun-deprived place.

Like its offline inspiration (Disney World), Toontown is designed to make kids feel that this is a space where they are in charge. Things like squirt guns and pies in the face are not only encouraged but specifically incorporated into the game as official battle tactics to be used against the Cogs. A kid-centered world does have its limits, however. Communication is limited to a drop-down menu of phrases called "Speed Chat". The only way to converse freely with someone in Toontown is to make them a "secret friend" which requires both parties to enter a password exchanged outside the game. This may limit the world's development as a social space, but it does ensure a higher level of safety.

Hello Kitty Online

http://www.hellokittyonline.com

Windows and Mac
Launch Date: Beta 2008
Target Audience: tweens to 20s
Revenue Model: promotional, in-world commerce

Hello Kitty has enjoyed an astounding licensing boom from children's toys to "grown-up" luxury items over the past several years with great success. It's therefore not a big surprise that the simply drawn white kitty has hew own 3D MMOPRG. Created by SanrioDigital and Typhoon Games it is a fun, cheerful and lighthearted cartoon world aimed at tween girls to young adult women. Along with the standard avatar/home/pet customization, Hello Kitty Online is an interesting mix of modern high tech meets traditional (and perhaps lost) skills by offering a potpourri of quests from conquering monsters to picking fruit from trees and farming to cooking, tailoring, making furniture, and building houses. The MMPORG is fully integrated with SanrioTown which offers Hello Kitty email, video sharing and editing, Sanriotown blogs, and of course games. Kitty Dollars is the in-world currency to spend on your character! Hello Kitty Online includes interaction with other favorite Sanrio characters such as My Melody, Pochacco, Badtz-Maru.

Lego Universe

http://www.legouniverse.com
Windows and Mac
Launch Date: Beta 2008
Target Audience: 8- to 12-year-olds
Revenue Model: subscription, promotional, links to on-line commerce

Lego Universe is a newer entry vw where Lego fans from around the globe create, build and play together (what else?)

a Lego-based virtual world. In Lego Universe, avatars are called "mini-figures" and Lego provides the basic skeleton for each themed "world" within the world. How those worlds are built up is all up to the users. Missions will abound but when mini-figures are injured or die, there are no worries about gratuitous gore – they'll just break apart. A blueprinting system is reported to be in the works so users can create and send plans of favorite creations on to friends or conversely keep the blueprint of the creation top secret.

While the world is aimed at 8- to 12-year-olds, the creators believe many adults will also be involved. The primary goal for the company is to create "a safe space MMO where kids can go to play comfortably without all the nonsense that many adult MMOs bring to the table." As such, Lego is backing the world with massive manpower by monitoring all text, chat and characters.

Millsberry

http://www.millsberry.com
Windows and Mac
Launch Date: 2004
Target Audience: 7- to 14-year-olds
Revenue Model: promotional, advertising

Millsberry is a 2D vw from General Mills that's rich in product placements as well as mini-games for Millsbucks, the in-world currency. Civic responsibility, nutrition and exercise are core themes throughout the world, and each character has five statistical attributes – Fitness, Civics, Health, Intelligence and Hunger – that can be affected and improved by in-game choices and participation levels. An arcade of games is also available.

Mokitown

http://www.mokitown.com
Windows and Mac
Launch Date: 2001
Target Audience: 8- to 12-year-olds
Revenue Model: promotional

Mokitown is a cartoon-like world built for children aged 8 to 12. Sponsored by DaimlerChrysler, Mokitown's goal is to educate its young members (called "mokis" – short for "mobile kids") about road and traffic safety through this shared social experience.

Mokis encounter virtual urban settings like street crossings and transportation venues that require them to make judgment calls about how to safely move about in the virtual space. A "quizbot" roams around Mokitown testing kids with traffic safety questions. Correct answers are rewarded with "mobility points" which can be redeemed for virtual items like avatar clothing, hairstyles, and other accessories. Unsafe or careless actions result in the deduction of points from a moki's account. The world is free to users and free of advertising.

Although mokis can chat freely with each other in the world, basic pre-formatted chat phrases like "how are you?" and "I like your outfit" are available for those at a loss for words. To obtain private chat functionality (i.e., instant messaging) mokis must purchase a "cell phone" with the points they've earned. The world is partially moderated by Mokitown staff.

Nicktropolis

http://www.nicktropolis.com

Windows and Mac
Launch Date: 2007
Target Audience: 6- to 14-year-olds (emphasis on 9- to 12-year-olds)
Revenue Model: promotional, advertising

Nicktropolis is Nick.com's immersive 3D world for kids to safely "hang-out, be creative and connect with each other online." Avatar customization, room decoration, virtual pets, chat rooms, NickPoints to buy stuff with, tons of games including treasure hunts, videos of Nickelodeon TV shows and interaction with Nickelodeon TV show characters such as SpongeBob SquarePants and Jimmy Neutron are among the chief features and highlights. The Slime Room at the Amusement Pier is among several interactive common rooms users can visit. Inside Nicktropolis, users can navigate different areas such as Downtown Nicktropolis, TeenNick Point, or Nicktoons Boulevard through a point-and-click map. Sub-areas are mostly Nickelodeon show based and include Naked Brothers Band Apartment, Jimmy Neutron's Retroville, and SpongeBob's Bikini Bottom. Within the world there are plenty of safety guidelines and precautions for both kids and parents' reference. There is also a "sanitized dictionary" of what is appropriate language for chat rooms. NickPoints are the in-world currency users earn by playing games or by finding hidden Nick "blobs" in various colors. Points can be redeemed to buy room décor and accessories as well as collector's cards.

ToppsTown

http://www.toppstown.com
Windows and Mac
Launch Date: 2008

Target Audience: 6-year-olds upwards
Revenue Model: retail products

Sports and collectible card maker Topps launched its first virtual world, Toppstown in 2008. Sporting the tag line "Where Your Cards Come Alive!" the world lets users create their own avatars, customize clubhouses, and collect and trade virtual cards. Users buy Topps packages of cards at retail stores and use the code provided (1 code in every 2 packs) to register. The codes are also given away as a promotional tool at events, in advertisements or in packaging from food product partners. Aimed at kids aged 6 and up, the world is reported to have little user interaction, but is very trading and game oriented. The look and feel of the world itself is much more teen-oriented despite its young target age.

vMTV

http://www.vmtv.com
Windows and Mac
Launch Date: 2007
Target Audience: ages 14 to 20s
Revenue Model: Premium subscription, sponsorships, advertising, product placement

vMTV is a portal to a collection of virtual worlds made up of actual MTV shows. The 2008 line-up includes: *Virtual Laguna Beach, The Virtual Hills, Virtual Pimp My Ride, Virtual Backstage Pass, Virtual Skate Park, Virtual America's Best Dance Crew, The Virtual Real World*. Users can also club-hop among hip neighborhoods, buy music, watch videos, sing karaoke, start a band and of course chat (code in this case for flirt).
    Note: vMTV and its collection of worlds are available both as stand-alone worlds and from within There.com

VIRTUAL WORLDS FOR KIDS/TWEENS ONLY

Beanie Babies 2.0

http://www.beaniebabies.ty.com
Windows and Mac
Launch Date: 2008
Target Audience: not specified
Revenue Model: retail products

Users buy their own Beanie Babies 2.0 plush toy and enter the scratch-off secret code to register. Once registered, users receive their own Beanie Babies 2.0 room to play in, make friends in chat rooms located at the community tree or in any one of the habitats (the Farm, the Fun Forest, the Backyard, or the Hole). Users can meet with "Mayor Bean" to receive updates and information regarding the site and also have access to play many different types of games testing players' skill, knowledge and memory. Each user receives their own profile page where they can manage their buddy list, create and display a family flag, and share their hobbies and interests. Users also receive a "Big Book of Beanies" to design and update his/her family's profile featuring individual pages for each Beanie Babies 2.0 that has been registered. Unlike Webkinz, US$6 toys have no expiration date on the subscription and premium levels can be claimed only by purchasing more plush toys.

Build-A-Bearville

http://www.buildabearville.com
Windows and Mac
Launch Date: 2008
Target Audience: 6- to 12-year-olds
Revenue Model: retail product, promotional

Build-A-Bear Workshop® is a retail store best known for giving children the opportunity to build and customize their very own stuffed bear friend. Build-A-Bearville takes this same concept and its core value of "friendship" and extends both to its own virtual world, where users once they purchase and customize their physical bear can create the virtual version in-world. The usual ingredients of avatars, chat, games, in-world stuff to purchase with points and socialization go into this world. Bear Bills are the in-world currency.

Disney Club Penguin (formerly Club Penguin)

http://www.clubpenguin.com
Windows and Mac
Launch Date: 2005
Target Audience: primary target is 6- to 14-year-olds but open to all
Revenue Model: subscription, in-world store merchandise, advertising, sponsorships

Acquired by Disney in 2007 for a reported US$700 million, users interact in a snowy playground using penguins as avatars. Users socialize, play mini-games, furnish and decorate their igloos, explore different snowy areas, and accessorize. Coins are the in-world currency and are earned through mini-games to buy furniture and accessories. Mini-games can also be educational. One of the mini-games, "Paint by Letters" is an engaging way to practise reading, spelling and keyboarding through creative storytelling. Buying is only available to paid subscription holders while free members may use the coins to buy general customizables, like penguin colors. For increased safety and parental control: "Club Penguin's parent features allow adults to logon and view their child's account history (including any bans and account payments), change their child's password and choose whether their child can chat by selecting from pre-approved phrases or by typing in their own messages. An integrated timer, which lets parents set the time of day and duration of their child's visit to Club Penguin, will be released later this month."

Dizzywood

http://www.dizzzywood.com
Windows and Mac
Launch Date: 2007
Target Audience: 8- to 12-year-olds
Revenue Model: Unknown

Dizzywood is a 3D, cartoonish virtual world for kids to customize avatars with clothes, items, e-motes and even super powers as well as play solo games or accomplish game challenges with others. Landscapes are varied such as the Mayan jungle. The world uses, as an interesting safety feature, a combination of automated filtering systems and live human moderators to assist kids from the temptation of revealing personal information online.

FusionFall (Cartoon Network Universe)

http://www.fusionfall.com
Windows and Mac
Launch Date: Beta 2008
Target Audience: 8- to 14-year-olds
Revenue Model: promotional, advertising, brand integration

FusionFall is the official virtual world for cable TV channel Cartoon Network. As the name implies, Cartoon Network is a 24/7 animation reflecting a variety of animation styles, genres and target ages. Combining a huge, mythical universe filled with ruins, mountains and giant futuristic skyscrapers (among other topographical features) with popular Cartoon Network show stars like Ben 10 and Billy and Mandy, the "nonstop" MMORPG charges players with defending the world from the villainous Fuse and his evil minions and is built to appeal to gamers and viewers alike. More than 50 Cartoon Network characters will be featured in the game. It is targeted at "kids of all ages."

HandiLand

http://www.handiland.com
Windows and Mac
Launch Date: Beta 2007
Target Audience: 4- to 12-year-olds
Revenue Model: premium subscription, in-world commerce

HandiLand is a virtual world offering kids "positive reinforcement and teaches the value of savings and work". HandiLand, which the company admits is "similar to Club Penguin and Webkinz", has 140,000 users from its Beta launch in November 2007, including 92,000 children aged 4 to 12, and 48,000 parents. Parents are encouraged to use the world as well, offering a "Parent Portal" which allows them to print out chore charts and reward certificates. If their children then do their real world chores, they earn points to spend on cartoons and games in HandiLand.

Littlest Pet Shop VIP

http://www.littlestpetshop.com
Windows and Mac
Launch Date: 2007

Target Audience: 8- to 12-year-olds
Revenue Mode: retail product, online commerce links

Hasbro's Littlest Pet Shop VIP (Virtual Interactive Pet) virtual world is designed for tween girls. Users first buy one or more miniature pets from the retail collection of plush animals. The toys have codes that unlock access to an online virtual world where each pet comes to life as a playful character. The 2008 version of the game includes significant enhancements including more games, activities and community features where girls and their VIPs can explore, nurture, exercise, "shop" and decorate. With well over 20 games and activities, the launch in nine languages is reported by the company to make it one of the largest global roll-out of a virtual world to date. Pileated Pictures, the same makers of Planet Cazmo (listed below), created the latest version of Littlest Pet Shop VIP. Online currency is (of course) called "kibble."

Lola's Land

http://www.lolasland.com
Windows and Mac
Launch Date: 2008
Target Audience: 9- to 13-year-olds
Revenue Model: promotional, advertising

Lola's Land is the first virtual world based on a series of books for young girls called the "Think Pink" series from publisher HarperCollins centered around the character of Lola Love. Created to promote author Lisa Clark's work, Lola's Land is the first of its kind from HarperCollins. The pink, chic cartoon world is a mix of social networking and virtual worlds, with customizable avatars, friend lists, games to earn spendable points, an interactive space, and daily updates for reviews, blogs, and celebrity news. The underlying message around Lola to tween girls is reported to be "having fun and feeling good about yourself."

MushABelly

http://www.mushabelly.com
Windows and Mac
Launch Date: 2007
Target Audience: not specified
Revenue Model: retail products

The MushABelly line are plush animals that double as "chattering, squeezable" pillows. Each MushABelly comes with its own game card and "Student ID Passcode" that allows its owner to enroll in MushABelly University within the accompanying virtual world. Along with the university, Mushabelly.com is a fantasy town for kids complete with stores and businesses such as the local barber shop, and pond. Animal sounds are plentiful such as an elephant, horse, kissing monkey, duck, and sheep. Kids can also read Che Che's stories, play Goldie's games and visit Rose's studio where they can paint. Although the products are meant to be for kids of all ages, the world is more focused on the very young (pre-school to lower elementary at most) based on its graphics, design and features.

Moshi Monsters

http://www.moshimonsters.com
Windows and Mac
Launch Date: Beta 2008
Target Audience: 7- to 12-year-olds
Revenue Model: retail product, premium subscription once launched publicly, merchandizing extensions planned

Moshi Monsters is an educational and social virtual world, taking a variation on the adopt-a-pet theme and offers users the chance to "adopt a monster." The cartoonish world corresponds to real world monster pets that come on a cell phone strap and light up when the phone rings. In-world Monsters are customizable and full of personality that becomes richer the more it's played with. Users nurture their little monster by solving daily puzzles and earning Rox, the in-world currency, redeemable for all sorts of food, furniture and trinkets for the monster. Puzzles are educational in nature and cover vocabulary, math, logic, spatial skills and other topics. More correct answers means more Rox. Puzzles are said to calibrate each day based on how the child is doing – well means increased difficulty, struggling means decreased. Monster blogs, newsfeeds, pinboards and buddy lists are among the networking features. Like the other kids vws, online safety is key.

Pixie Hollow(Disney Fairies)

http://disney.go.com/fairies/pixiehollow/comingSoon.html
Windows and Mac
Launch Date: Beta 2008
Target Audience: 4- to 12-year-olds
Revenue Model: premium subscription, links to online commerce, in-world commerce, promotional

Dubbed the most beautiful tiny world imaginable, Disney Fairies Pixie Hollow lives up to its hyped billing by using the same animation art styles that made Disney so famous mixed with beautiful original orchestral music and applying it to the fairy-filled (including Tinker Bell) vw aimed at young girls. Avatar customization, quizzes, mini-games, crafts, socializing and flying are among the key features. Female Disney fans of all ages are sure to fall for Pixie Hollow.

Planet VTech

http://www.planetvtech.com
Windows and Mac
Launch Date: Beta 2008
Target Audience: 5- to 11-year-olds
Revenue Model: retail products, premium subscription planned

VTech, the maker of educational electronic toys for young children, is launching its own virtual world Planet VTech that involves several of its learning laptops and handhelds, that connect to the Internet via USB, so that children can access Planet VTech as well. Games are central with players earning points that can be redeemed for "great rewards."

Socialization is a part of the world with safety caveats in place. The world is also intended to promote VTech's other products. The tie-in products are reported to come with a free one-year membership to Planet VTech, but there is no word how much a subsequent subscription will cost.

Playdo

http://www.playdo.com
Windows Only
Launch Date: 2000, Playdo 2.0 Beta 2006
Target Audience: unspecified
Revenue Model: unknown

Originally a graphical chat world, Playdo 2.0 has evolved into a cartoon-based, friends' community spanning over 150 countries with a focus on games, entertainment and social networking. On the website, all members "create their own profiles and citizens and take up residence in a fantastic world, full of friendly people and fun things to do . . . Playdo's latest product is the adventure world called Spine

World, in which the users and their avatars take residence, travel, chat and go on quests in a safe and cheerful monitored environment. Playdo also develops games and exclusive new technology for entertainment online."

Playdo claims its place as a well-known brand in the world of Internet communities. Founded in 1999 as a student research project, Playdo won multiple awards and influenced many other communities with its avatar chat world and pixel graphics. The company currently focuses on mobile access to the world.

Shining Stars

http://www.shiningstars.com
Windows and Mac
Launch Date: 2007
Target Audience: not specified
Revenue Model: retail products, premium subscription

Shining Stars follows the Neopets, Barbie.com, Webkinz model of a retail purchase of a Russ produced plush (stuffed) animal toy to enter the world of Shining Stars. Buyers will not only get the stuffed animal, but a chance to have a literal star in the sky named after him/her. Limited edition animals are occasionally available such as the Shining Star E.T. (character from the famous 1980s Universal movie) through the Universal Studios Theme Park and by mail order.

Once registered, the site shows an image and coordinates of the user's star that can be printed on a certificate to verify its exact location in space. E-cards, games and activities are among the world's other features.

Stardoll

http://www.stardoll.com

Windows and Mac
Launch Date: 2006
Target Audience: 7- to 17-year-olds
Revenue Model: in-world commerce, advertising, brand placement, brand integration

With the tag line "Fame, Fashion and Friends," Stardoll is a vw based in Stockholm, Sweden that leverages girls' fascinations with celebrities, fashion and socializing. Users dress up an impressive selection of celebrity dolls (essentially virtual paper dolls) resembling Jessica Alba to Usher to royalty and super models (and even US Late-Night host Conan O'Brian) with all sorts of different virtual clothes. Fancier virtual duds cost beyond the basic free membership price. As of 2008, the company claims 16 million plus users. In addition to teenage girls, the site has another surprising audience – their mothers. 81% of mothers are reported to visit Stardoll weekly and 63% visit the site without their daughter.

VizWoz

http://www.vizwoz.com
Windows only
Launch Date: 2008
Target Audience: 11- to 14-year-olds
Revenue Model: premium subscription, advertising, sponsorships, brand integration

VizWoz is a UK-based virtual world primarily based around its premium VIP services. For £2.95 per month, VIP members can access the DJ Studio consisting of four rooms catering to different genres of music and where members can mix their own tracks. A VizWoz DJ of the Year 2008 competition is also planned as is a virtual cinema. The cinema concept is already used by Gaia Online with their partnership with Sony and Warner Bros launched back in December 2007. As of this writing, media partners for the Vizwoz cinema have not been announced. Aside from music and movies, VizWoz caters for various tween/early teen tastes and interests including sport and fashion. It is the first virtual world to have its very own police force dubbed the "VizCops."

WebbliWorld

http://www.webbliworld.com
Windows and Mac
Launch Date: 2008
Target Audience: 6- to 12-year-olds
Revenue Model: sponsorships, brand integration

WebbliWorld is an imaginative and creatively drawn 2D world for kids around the globe to learn, explore and socialize from Aardman Animations, the creators of the British claymation series *Wallace and Gromit*. On the site, WebbliWorld "mirrors the real world and guides children through the mind-boggling maze of the Internet. Our friendly characters introduce important topics such as the environment, climate change and recycling in an accessible and memorable way. Here, kids will learn without even knowing it! We are working in partnership with WWF (World Wildlife Fund) to make sure that all our environmental messages are accurate and educational." The world also has a partnership with Puffin Books to showcase and review their new publications. The world also tackles "green" issues and the environment by rewarding users for making the "right" choices such as choosing eco-smart materials for building their Pod, switching off lights, conserving water, etc. The Webbli rainforest reflects how personal choices impact the environment, as is the WebbliBank, where kids can withdraw the in-world currency "Webbles" from ATMs with a PIN, and learn about saving money and even third world debt.

Webkinz

http://www.webkinz.com
Windows and Mac
Launch Date: 2005
Target Audience: 8- to 13-year-olds
Revenue Model: retail products, premium subscription

One of the first brands to marry real world toy purchases and a virtual world experience, members buy their Webkinz pet in a local retail store and then completes the purchase (and experience) by registering in the Webkinz virtual world with the product's unique "secret code" to customize the Webkinz pet's living space, play games and socialize. Created by Ganz (the makers of Beanie Babies), each pet costs between US$10 and US$20.

Whyville

http://www.whyville.net
Windows and Mac
Launch Date: 1999
Target Audience: tweens and teens aged 10 to 16.
Revenue Model: Premium access passes, sponsorships

Whyville is an educational virtual world for tweens and early teens, particularly girls aged between 8 and 15. Originally established to support an *LA Times* weekly science education article, this world's motto is "learning by doing." True to its word, Whyville actively engages its visitors and encourages them to participate in fun, educational events that give kids "hands-on" experience with science projects (in a virtual way, of course). Whyville citizens learn about art history, science, journalism, civics, economics, and more, working directly with the Getty, NASA, the School Nutrition Association, Woods Hole Oceanographic Institution, and other non-profit entities with outreach missions to create educational content for kids that's engaging.

While Whyville is partially moderated with a language filter and a staff of "city workers," the chat is not monitored 24/7. Current sponsors include Getty, NASA and Sun Microsystems.

Membership is free but Whyville offers its own VIP priority access pass to get into busy areas of Whyville and have extra perks, such as larger satchels and address book, non-expiring face parts, full-time access to Akbar's Face Factory, and priority access to special events.

WoogiWorld

http://www.woogiworld.com
Windows and Mac
Launch Date: 2007
Target Audience: 6- to 12-year-olds
Revenue Model: unknown

WoogiWorld wants to take Internet safety, manners and habits to a new level by teaching elementary age children worldwide how to become responsible Internet users and global goodwill ambassadors. The world's goal is to be the "tool of choice" that both parents and educators use to teach kids:

1. Proper, positive character traits and skills that include:
   - Internet behavior and safety (anti-bullying);
   - leadership;
   - service to others;
   - proper health and nutrition.

2. Balance between time on and off the Internet.
3. The value and benefit of actively participating in the community.

Features include games, trading cards, virtual pets, and of course, socialization.

ZooKazoo

http://www.zookazoo.com
Windows and Mac
Launch Date: 2008
Target Audience: 6- to 12-year-olds
Revenue Model: premium subscription, in-world commerce

For younger children of both genders, ZooKazoo is most like Disney Club Penguin but more educationally-oriented, with games that involve sorting objects and saving the environment. The almost old-fashioned like cartoon design environment is full of places to visit.

Users can add friends to their buddy list and earn money by playing games to purchase furniture, décor, clothing, for the user's "Zelf" (i.e., avatar). Entrance is free but premium games require subscription available for US$5.95 per month. In addition to the usual safety precautions for children-based worlds, ZooKazoo implements measures that make it impossible for anyone to use email to contact children from the world and never allow private communications between two users within the world.

Other worlds targeted at children only:

Disney Cars

In planning

Disney Pirates of the Caribbean

http://apps.pirates.go.com/pirates/v3/welcome

Go Pets

http://www.gopetslive.com

i-Citizen

Downloadable freeware

MyePets

http://www.myepets.com

Tech Deck Live

http://www.techdecklive.com

Whyworld Spain

In planning

VIRTUAL WORLDS FOR TEENS ONLY

DUBIT

http://www.dubit.co.uk/
Windows and Mac
Launch Date: 2001
Target Audience: teens (although officially 7- to 24-year-olds)
Revenue Model: advertising, product/brand promotions, sponsorships

According to the site Dubit is a free online community for UK teenagers, but the official target age (also according to the site) is 7- to 24-year-olds. Its virtual world, called "dubitisland 3D Chat," is just one of several social networking features including message boards, IM, blogs, and sponsored games and competitions. One thing you'll notice right away about Dubit is its heavy emphasis on corporate sponsorship. Advertisements for various movies, services, and products dominate the website, the chat rooms, and even the instant messages used by members. In fact, there are so many ads that the site appears to exist solely to market various brands to teenage customers. Members are encouraged to sign up as "informers" to keep the company apprised of marketing trends and are even recruited to help advertise products and services to their friends through the Dubit Brand Street Teams in exchange for prizes and cash. Dr. Pepper, Coke, and Bic are among the larger brands currently represented by the teams. It also offers the "DubitCard" as a free V.I.P. card to members for real world store/partner discounts within the U.K.

According to Betsy Book, one of the beautiful ironies of Dubit is that within this ultra-commercial space of movie and Pizza Hut promotions exists one of the nicest, most mature and charming, close-knit communities of teens online. While in-world advertising is certainly more prevalent in Dubit, the absence of an in-world economy means that this community's focus is more on socializing rather than buying/selling/earning virtual goods.

Habbo (formerly Habbo Hotel)

http://www.habbo.com (accesses US site)
Windows and Mac
Launch Date: 2001
Target Audience: 13- to 17-year-olds

Revenue Model: subscription, advertising

Habbo (formerly Habbo Hotel) is the largest global virtual hang-out for teens, created by Finnish company, Sulake Labs. This busy site uses a hotel metaphor as its theme complete with a "lobby" gateway and private "guest rooms." The hotels are often so busy it can take a few tries to get into the main rooms, but there are always a plenty of guest rooms to choose from as well.

Guest rooms can be decorated with furniture (or "furni" as Habbos call it) purchased with "Habbo credits." Habbo credits can be purchased with several types of RL currency (UK Pounds sterling, Euros, US dollars, Canadian dollars, and Australian dollars) in a wide variety of ways (credit card, mobile phone, prepaid stored value cards). Furni may set you back a few credits, but access to the world itself is free and relatively easy to navigate. Cool new additions to the Habbo catalogue include pets and pet accessories.

As of April 2008, Double Fusion, an independent in-game advertising firm, is the exclusive advertising sales agency for the Habbo.com property in the US. According to a Habbo press release, "Double Fusion will work with advertisers from the entertainment industry, retail, fashion and sports arenas to create relevant and interactive brand campaigns. By integrating branding elements into its virtual world, Habbo builds exposure and increases awareness without the use of intrusive ads. The partnership aims to build campaigns that support the Habbo experience, and that organically grow due to the community support."

Habbo is an international phenomenon with several other versions for residents of 32 countries, including the United Kingdom, Finland, Japan, Switzerland, Spain, Italy, Sweden and China.

ourWorld

http://www.ourworld.com
Windows and Mac
Launch Date: Beta 2008
Target Audience: 11- to 15-year-olds
Revenue Model: premium subscription, partnerships

ourWorld is a 2D animation/anime avatar based virtual world. ourWorld is billed a casual, social gaming site where kids play on-line games, win ourWorld money and prizes, create and personalize their character and socialize with their friends as well as take in-game jobs. Parents have the control to decide the level of the child's interaction within the world. By playing games users earn "Flow" – the energy that runs ourWorld. The more Flow means the more spins earned on the prize wheel, where users win ourWorld money, clothing, and accessories. ourWorld claims to be an "island in the sky created by a group of kids who were tired of the mundane world and wanted to create a world that expressed their creativity and imagination." The Boardwalk and Pier areas, Buzz café, Starlight Lounge for dancing, Sideshow for watching YouTube videos are among the chief places to visit.

Planet Cazmo

http://www.planetcazmo.com
Windows and Mac
Launch Date: Beta 2008
Target Audience: tweens to teens
Revenue Model: premium subscription, Planet Cazmo branded products

Planet Cazmo is an original virtual world creation by Pileated Pictures aimed at tweens and teens. Along with the usual characteristics of an avatar-based virtual world, this new in 2008 world offers mini-games and the ability to create in-game content and games. Players can buy things within the in-world store and trade items with one another as well.

SmallWorlds

http://www.smallworlds.com
Windows and Mac
Launch Date: Beta 2008
Target Audience: 11- to 18-year-olds plus
Revenue Model: *advertising, premium subscriptions*

SmallWorlds is a web-based (versus downloadable client based) 3D virtual world with customizable avatars that are more reminiscent of Toy Story than say Second Life. Room customization and chatting with friends is standard as is playing games from pool (billiards) to old-school arcade games and watching YouTube videos together on "flat screen TVs." For the official launch, the company will be adding premium accounts which give access to other features such as virtual pets, instant messaging and voice chat client, and more. Outsmart is the software-development company behind SmallWorlds and is based in Auckland, New Zealand with an office in Los Angeles. The virtual world is English-speaking based and will be targeting Asian countries in the near future.

vSide

http://www.vside.com
Windows and Mac
Launch Date: 2008
Target Audience: 13- to 24-year-olds
Revenue Model: advertising, product placement/brand integration, sponsorships

vSide describes itself as a totally immersive 3D world with "international flair" providing teens with a complement to their existing 2D, text-based social networking pages and focused on music, fashion and socializing. Users create and dress an avatar, furnish their apartments, move about in-world and interact with friends in real-time, listen to a broad compilation of music, take in all the latest fashions from the hottest brands and party with friends in their own personal spaces. Complementing the virtual world, vSide also features its own website which serves as a way for teens to communicate their in-world vSide activity to their friends through their social network of choice, such as Facebook and MySpace. The website empowers users to manage their in-world profiles, track currency (called vBux), publish vSide photographs, and more.

Whirled

http://www.whirled.com/
Windows and Mac
Launch Date: 2008
Target Audience: teens
Revenue Model: in-world commerce, brand integration

Whirled is a teen-targeted MMO created by Three Rings, the same makers of Puzzle Pirates and has been compared to The Palace (see 2D chat rooms below). Within its 2D cartoon environment, Whirled offers player-created content and social interaction over character development and time-consuming quests. A Flash-based interface allows for easy creation of items, furniture, avatars, and even complex multiplayer games. A system is in place that allows users to flag and block inappropriate content.

WhyRobbieRocks

http://www.whyrobbierocks.com

Windows and Mac
Launch Date: 2003
Target Audience: 12- to 20-year-olds
Revenue Model: brand promotions, advertising, sponsorships, in-world commerce

WhyRobbieRocks is a 2D avatar driven fashion world aimed at 12- to 20-year-olds with the ability to play with avatars that function as virtual "paper dolls." WRR taps into celebrity culture by offering pre-made avatars that resemble popular celebs, including Justin Timberlake, Beyonce, J-Lo, Orlando Bloom, and Paris Hilton. Members are also encouraged to create their own unique looks which can be individualized with a wide variety of trendy clothing and accessories. Dressed-to-the-nines avatars can interact in glamorous social settings like pool, beach, and lounge areas or the cityscape or country-themed rooms, which are a mix of graphic illustrations and photographic backgrounds. On the newly styled WRR, members can make an avatar for free, styled from more than 5,000 items including from brands such as Eastpak, Ugg and Diesel. Members can also design their own clothes and accessories, and make their own shop to sell/promote items or the ones from famous brands available in-world.

Other virtual worlds targeted to teens only:

Teen Second Life

http://teen.secondlife.com

Awteen

http://www.awteen.com

2D VIRTUAL WORLD CHAT COMMUNITIES

The Manor

http://community.madwolfsw.com
Windows and Mac
Launch Date: 2006
Target Audience: kids to mature adults
Revenue Model: unknown

The Manor dubs itself as a 2D virtual chat community for everyone. Created by a lone engineer with the statement "The Manor isn't backed by some big corporation, just one slightly touched engineer with a dream and his family" (*Scotsman*). The "Manorverse" is for friends to talk to friends (old, new or virtual) in unique and private settings. The Manor states that privacy is a key concern and automatically sets accounts to a private profile. Members can switch their profile to public upon request. Kids' controls are also available to parents. The world functions from downloadable software created by Mad Wolf Software.

The Palace

http://www.thepalace.com
Windows only
Launch Date: 1995
Target Audience: all ages
Revenue Model: unknown

Originally developed by Jim Bumgardner for Time Warner Interactive in 1995, The Palace software has since been owned and developed by several failed companies, the last of which (Communities.com) disappeared in 2001. In spite of this, hundreds of palaces happily live on, maintained by dedicated palace citizen volunteers (with no affiliation to Communities.com) across a network of palace servers. The task of developing The Palace's successor has been attempted several times, but most notably by The Manor.

The Palace software provides a visual 2D chat space with ambience created by photos and original artworks that serve more as scenic backdrops than any realistic illusion of space. The Palace's greatest feature is its ability to allow users to create avatars out of any image imaginable, creating endless opportunities for self-expression. A palace exists for just about every theme, topic, and demographic imaginable. A list of featured palaces is available at: www.thepalace.com.

Voodoo Chat

http://www.voodoochat.com
Windows Only
Launch Date: 2001
Target Audience: 18-year-olds upwards
Revenue Model: unknown

Voodoo Chat is a free 2D graphical chat space similar in nature to The Palace. Like The Palace, it is now being administered by its community members on a collection of independent servers. Access is free to anyone willing to download and install the software. Voodoo Chat visitors can customize their avatars from any GIF, BMP, JPG, or PNG file they wish to use.

Voodoo Chat visitors are generally friendly and welcoming, and the atmosphere in Voodoo Chat rooms is laid-back and casual. According to its website, Voodoo Chat is "a collection of privately owned and operated servers, each of which has its own set of rules, or no rules at all." As a result, many of the Voodoo Chat servers and rooms feature "adult" content, making many of these environments most suitable for those over the age of 18. However, each Voodoo Chat has its own distinct style and rules, with themes ranging from Anime to Poetry, so interested visitors may want to browse a bit before settling on one destination.

Features include animated graphics, voice chatting, interactive games, and the ability to run your own server.

VPchat

http://www.vpchat.com
Windows only
Launch Date: 2001
Target Audience: all
Revenue Model: premium subscription

A 2D chat space that uses Virtual Places chat software, VPchat was founded in 2001 by two former Excite community developers, Tom Lang and Julie Gomoll. Like The Palace, VPchat is comprised of a 2D network of widely varying virtual worlds. Each world contains a set of rooms with background images and 2D avatar-based communication via chat bubbles, gestures, and sounds.

Most VPchat members came to the service via Virtual Places and represent a wide variety of interests and age ranges. Most of them are from the United States. A favorite activity in VPchat spaces is group participation in online versions of traditional board games like backgammon, checkers, and Yahtzee. VPChat strives for and prides itself on being free of advertising.

3D VIRTUAL WORLD CHAT COMMUNITIES

IMVU

http://www.imvu.com

Windows only
Launch Date: 2004
Target Audience: 13-year-olds upwards
Revenue Model: advertising, premium membership, in-world commerce

IMVU is actually not a virtual world in the strictest sense but rather a 3D Instant Messaging (IM) client offering users a customizable 3D avatar and chat service through a downloadable application. A customizable homepage is also offered to users. Avatars have plenty of clothes, accessories and scenes to choose from. While each scene looks like part of a full virtual world, movement within the scenes is limited when compared to worlds like Second Life. IMVU has a younger user base but certain content is deemed "restricted" and available to users over the age of 18. Age verification was more recently added. IMVU plans to add games, branded accessories, and characters to the program. Users will be able to be their favorite movie stars and dress in clothes they wear in real life. This potentially opens IMVU up to clothing and accessory advertisers as well as game developers.

MMORPGs

Entropia

http://www.entropia.com
Windows only
Launch date: 2003
Target Audience: 18-year-olds upwards
Revenue Model: in-world currency and economy

In the Entropia Universe realistic looking 3D futuristic themes take place on the planet Calypso, where users play the role of "settlers" to explore and colonize the land, hunt monsters for trading and selling purposes, mine for materials to form new civilizations within Calypso.

Entropia is an MMORPG that is free to play but with a real cash economy. PED, the world's virtual currency has a fixed exchange rate to the US$ (10 Entropia dollars is 1 US$) that can be both deposited and withdrawn as virtual/real world money. Successful gamers are reported to therefore make real money by playing – a bit of a mix between World of Warcraft with Second Life. Entropia's website states that, "the Entropia Universe is a direct continuation of Project Entropia, which had a 2006 turnover of 3.6 billion PED ($360 million)"

MapleStory

http://www.maplestory.com
Windows only
Launch date: 2003
Target Audience: 13-year-olds upwards
Revenue Model: In-world currency and commerce, product extensions

MapleStory is a 2D, free to play MMO with worlds to explore and quests to fulfill. In addition to the classic role-playing, goal-oriented game structure, there is social interaction through chatting, trading, and playing mini-games. Groups of players can band together in parties to hunt monsters, share the rewards, and join guilds. The Cash Shop, the main *Revenue Model*, is the world's virtual shop featuring pets, modeled on monkeys, dogs, cats, bunnies, pandas, pigs, etc. that follow the owner around. An interesting feature is that it levies in-game virtual taxes. (Big Brother is everywhere.) Begun in Korea, MapleStory is taking over the rest of the world and has successfully spawned an anime show in Japan and Nintendo DS game. The Korean version, as the first to be created, it is reported to offer the most features compared to later versions in North America and Europe.

In addition to the worlds in the guide above, Massively.com lists the following MMOPRGs currently active in the marketplace:

TowerChat

http://www.towerchat.co.uk
Windows and Mac
Launch Date: 2000
Target Audience: all, but with an emphasis on teens
Revenue Model: banner ads, ads by Google, news ticker advertising

TowerChat is a UK-based 3D chat service. Public environments are divided into eight subject "towers" including Politics, Music, and Love. The avatar choices are attractive males or attractive females (but no non-human avatars). Based on this and the "singles nightclub" feel of the world, the main focus of TowerChat activity seems to be flirting with the opposite sex. This theme is reinforced by the fact that three of the eight towers are labeled "Love Chat," "Flirting Chat," and "Romantic Chat" and the rooms within each tower have names like "Penthouse," "London Boozer," "Carefree Bar," and simply "Bar."

TowerChat caters to UK teens, who are its most frequent visitors. In addition, TowerChat is offered as a customizable virtual chat room for any website without any "in-depth modifications." Additional space for chat room software installation, third-party module downloads and extra personnel are eliminated with the TowerChat as the chat room is hosted on TowerChat's servers and modifiable to each unique brand. A customized TowerChat application already exists for fans of the Chelsea UK football team: http://chelsea.towerchat.com/

Additional MMORPGs

2Moons
Age of Conan
Aion
Albatross 18
All Points Bulletin
Anarchy Online
Animal Crossing
ArchLord
Arden
Asheron's Call
Battlefield Heroes
Blackstar
Blue Mars
Bounty Bay Online
Cabal Online
Champions Online
Chronicles of Spellborn
City of Heroes
City of Villains
Corum Online
CrimeCraft
Dark Age of Camelot
DarkEden Online
Darkfall
Dekaron
Dofus
Dream of Mirror Online
Dreamlords
Dungeon Runners
Dungeons and Dragons
   Online
Earth Eternal

Earthrise
Empire of Sports
Eternal Lands
Eudemons Online
EVE Online
EverQuest
EverQuest II
Everquest Online Adventures
Exanimus
Exteel
Face of Mankind
Fallen Earth
Fiesta
Final Fantasy XI
Flyff
Football Manager Live
Freaky Creatures
Free Realms
Fury
FusionFall
Global Agenda
Gods and Heroes
Godswar Online
Grand Chase
Guild Wars
Guild Wars 2
Hellgate: London
Hero Online
Holic
Home
Horizons
Huxley

Irth Worlds
Jumpgate
Jumpgate Evolution
Kingdom of Loathing
Kingdom Under Fire
Knight Online
Last Chaos
Legend of Mir: The Three
Heroes
Lineage
Lineage 2
Lord of the Rings Online
Love
Mabinogi
MagiKnights
Marvel Universe Online
Meridian 59
MetaPlace
Might and Magic
Minions of Mirth
Mortal Online
MU Online
Myst Online: URU Live
Myth War Online
Mythos
Neocron 2
Nexus: The Kingdoms of the
  Winds
Oberin
Perfect World
Phantasy Star Universe
Pirates of the Burning Sea
Pirates of the Caribbean Online
PlanetSide

PlayStation Home
PMOG
Priston Tale
Puzzle Pirates
Ragnarok Online
Rappelz
Requiem: Bloodymare
RF Online
Runescape
Ryzom
Saga
Scions of Fate
Secret of the Solstice
Shadowbane
Sho Online
Silkroad Online
Snow Crash
Star Trek Online
Star Wars Galaxies
Stargate Worlds
Stone Age 2
Sword of the New World
Tabula Rasa
Tales of Pirates
The Agency
The Chronicles of Spellborn
The Day
The Matrix Online
The Realm Online
The Secret World
The Sims Online
Trickster Online
Ultima Online
Vanguard

Vastpark
Vendetta Online
Virtual World
Voyage Century Online
Wakfu
Warhammer 40k
Warhammer Online
Warlords Online
Warrior Epic

Wizard101
World of Darkness
World of Kung Fu
World of Pirates
World of Warcraft
Wurm Online
WWIIOL: Battleground Europe
Zhengtu Online
Zu Online

Sources

http://www.massively.com/category/virtual worlds/
http://www.worldsinmotion.biz/atlas/

GLOSSARY OF TERMS

2D: Two-dimensional. Looking at a computer screen, television screen or printed magazine are examples of two-dimensional experiences.

3D: Three-dimensional. The addition of depth to a visual picture or representation.

Ad Farm: A tiny parcel of land that features advertising images floating on or above it.

Advergame: An electronic game that is designed to promote a product or a brand.

AJAX: Acronym for synchronous JavaScript and XML which is a web development technique for creating interactive web applications.

ALT: Abbreviation of alternative account which is when a user holds more than one membership account.

Av, Avie: Abbreviation for avatar.

Avatar: A term from Hindu mythology for the temporary body a god inhabits while visiting Earth. In virtual worlds, an avatar is a visual representation of the user that interacts in the world.

Avatar Customization: The ability to personalize how a user wants his/her avatar to look based on the options offered by the individual virtual world. Hair, eyes, make-up, clothing, height, weight, and facial features are all examples of what can typically be customized.

Avatar Teleport/AV Port: A central area where avatars can travel between worlds or a room or large projection space where avatars can interact with others in a real physical gathering.

Banishment: A severe consequence to violations of in-world rules where the user is expelled from the world and forbidden to return.

Banner Ad: A rectangular advertisement placed on a website. Clicking on the ad links back to the advertiser's own website or a relevant landing page.

Beta: Phase of software development that is more advanced than the initial alpha version. This phase is used to test for final bugs/glitches before final release to the general public.

Black Sun: The name of the dance club featured prominently in Neal Stephenson's 1992 sci fi novel *Snow Crash*.

Blog: An online journal that is frequently updated and publicly available on the web. **Blogger:** is the person who keeps an online journal.

Blogosphere: is the collective of blogs on the Internet.

Body Parts: Components or pieces that construct the physical appearance of an avatar.

Brand: A composition of tangible and intangible attributes, name and visual look that represents a company, product, service, technology. When managed properly creates value and influence.

Brand Awareness: The act of presenting a specific brand in order to maximize its recognition; the actual top-of-mind response of the brand by a consumer or group of consumers.

Brand Essence: A brand's promise expressed in the simplest, most concise terms. Examples include: Disney = magic; Volvo = safety.

Brand Experience: The interaction between brand and consumer at all points in the marketing/marketplace and how it is processed and received by the consumer.

Brand Extension: A brand that is extended into new markets, products, services, etc. by leveraging the brand's core attributes.

Brand Identity: The outward focused representation of the brand including its name and logo.

Brand Image: How the brand is received and perceived by a consumer or the marketplace.

Brand Proposition: The central promise a brand makes to its customers. The brand proposition should be appealing, easily understood and relevant to the target market.

Browser: A type of software program used to communicate with servers to obtain and view information through the Internet. Examples are Firefox, Safari, Explorer, etc.

Camera Position: A scene's viewpoint within a world. Users can change camera positions to adjust the viewpoint to different angles.

Chat Room: An area for users to congregate in order to communicate with one another. Conversations are typically textually based (i.e., typed in) and can be read by everyone present.

Click Through: The process of clicking through an online advertisement to the advertiser's destination.

Client Program: Software that is typically downloaded from the Internet to a user's computer that can communicate with other servers on the Internet. Examples of virtual world client programs are There.com and Second Life's client programs downloaded onto a user's computer in order to interact within the respective worlds.

Client/Server Network: A number of client programs linked together to communicate with each other through central servers.

Clothing/Virtual Clothing: Jacket, shirt, pants, undershirt, underpants, gloves, socks, shoes, skirt, etc. worn on top of its body and typically chosen and purchased by the user.

Collaboration: The ability to communicate and interact with people across physical and temporal boundaries by sharing information through different online mediums such as email, blogs, forums, chat rooms, podcasts, websites, virtual worlds and various social networking sites.

Community Standards: See **Terms of Service**

COPPA: Acronym for Children's Online Privacy Protection Act passed by the US Congress in 1998.

Counterfeit Brands/Products: Unofficial, illegal copies of branded products made by third-parties to sell for profit.

Creative Commons: A non-profit organization that seeks to expand how intellectual property is available for others to use legally.

Customer Touch Points: All of the physical, communication and human interactions that customers experience with a brand.

Cyberspace: A term coined by author William Gibson in his 1984 novel *Neuromancer* that references a futuristic computer network people use by plugging their minds into it. The term now refers to the Internet or to the online or digital world in general.

Demographics: The description of a group of people's characteristics, such as age, sex, nationality, marital status, education, occupation or income.

Differentiator: Any tangible or intangible characteristic that can be used to distinguish a product or a company from other products and companies, related to **differentiation**.

Digital Rights Management/DRM: A software platform/system that protects the copyright of data and forbids or limits sharing data circulated on the Internet.

Disruptive Technology: A new technology that unexpectedly displaces an established technology; coined by Harvard professor Clayton M. Christensen in 1997.

DOT COM (.COM): A company that operates on the web.

DOT EDU (.EDU): An educational institution that operates on the web.

DOT GOV (.GOV): A government agency that operates on the web.

DOT ORG (.ORG): A non-profit organization that operates on the web.

EUALA: Acronym for "End User Access and Licensing Agreement."

Emoticon: Symbol created either with punctuation keys on the computer keyboard or graphically produced to express an emotion. Examples are: :) smiley face ;) winking.

Event: A group activity, led by a host, that starts and ends at a specific time.

Fair Use: The legal guidelines which exempt educators from certain copyright restrictions.

Flying: An in-world action that allows an avatar to soar through the sky in order to move from place to place more quickly. (Think Superman.)

Gesture: A physical expression by an avatar using facial or body movement. Examples are winking, blowing a kiss, waving, etc.

Grid: A collection of SIMs (virtual land). In Second Life, Linden Lab provides the grid, and residents build the superstructure and surface infrastructure. Also known as **farm**.

Griefer: An avatar who is harassing others by using offensive language, bumping, etc. to intentionally disrupt or harm another user.

Handle: Name created to represent the user on the screen. Also referred to as an alias.

Haptic Technology: The sense of touch within a computer-generated environment.

Home: A place chosen to return to if a user becomes disoriented while traveling. Home is also the name of Sony Playstation's virtual world.

Impression: Produced when a user sees/views an online ad or web page.

Instant Message/IM: A private, one-to-one message sent to a specific person while in-world. Not the same as chat.

In-world: The state of being present within a virtual world (versus the real world).

In-world Economy: An infrastructure of virtual world currency, commerce and financial tracking available to users sometimes linked to real world cash and currencies.

In-world Commerce: The actual buying and selling of goods and services within a virtual world.

IRL: Acronym for "in real life."

Island: A sim/region that is detached from the main continent and accessible by directly teleporting to it.

Land Baron: A resident of Second Life who owns a significant quantity of land, especially with the intent of selling it at a profit.

Land Owner: A user who owns land; from a parcel of land to multiple estates.

Landmark: Coordinates to a location in-world.

Lindens, Linden dollars, L$: The official currency of Second Life.

LindeX: Linden dollar market exchange unique to Second Life.

Logo: A visual symbol used to represent a company, product or service that is typically legally protected.

Market Segmentation: The process of dividing the total market into smaller sections based on shared characteristics.

Mashups: A technology, service or company that was created by combining two or more existing concepts to create an entirely new entity.

Metabrand: A brand that is within a virtual world.

Metabranding: The act of branding and having a brand presence within a virtual world.

Metaverse: Term from Author Neal Stephenson's sci fi novel *Snow Crash* to signify a large virtual world in cyberspace.

Microtransactions: Small, low cost commerce transactions typically quantified by pennies.

Mini-game: A short video game often contained within another game. Sometimes referred to as a **subgame**.

Mirror World: A literal digital representation of the real world that attempts to map (or mirror) real world structures in 2D or 3D forms. Example: Google Earth.

MMORPG: Abbreviation for Massively Multi-Player Online Role Playing Game.

MMO: Alternative abbreviation for MMORPG.

MUD: Abbreviation for Multi User Domain or Dungeon which is a text chat-based virtual world set up for role-playing games.

Narrowcasting: The production of media content that targets a highly specific segment of the audience. The opposite of broadcasting.

Newbie: A new user of anything, including virtual worlds.

Notecard: A small text file within Second Life sometimes with embedded pictures, landmarks, or objects that can be given to avatars.

Object: 3D shapes within a virtual world: a user can possess and/or interact with.

Online Privacy: The handling and protection of sensitive personal information on the Internet.

Open Source Software: Software developed in a public, collaborative manner whose license permits users to study, change, improve and share the software, in a modified or unmodified form.

Parcel: An area of land owned by a single user or group. Parcels are composed of square blocks measuring 4×4 meters, but the blocks do not have to be contiguous.

Personal Broadcasting: Individually-produced content made available to others via the Internet. Examples are blogs and video clips available on YouTube.

Photo Realistic/Photo Realism: An attempt to create authentic looking images with great detail and texture.

Podcasting: A method for delivering audio or video files to users who subscribe to them either free or for a fee.

Portal: Polygons or icons that a user can pass through in a virtual space to automatically load a new world or execute a user-defined function.

Premium Subscription: A increased subscription, paid by some users, that has more privileges than the basic membership costs and basic perks.

PRIM: Abbreviation for "primitive" meaning a 3D object represented by a set of parameters, including position, scale, rotation, shape, cut, hollow, etc. that can be linked together into sets.

Product Placement: The appearance of a brand and/or product in TV shows, movies and video games as part of the content.

Profile: Information provided by and about a user that can generally be viewed by other users; may include a picture, biographical information, etc.

Properties: Denotes the action capabilities of an object or avatar.

Psychographics: The definition of consumers or audience members on the basis of psychological characteristics and traits.

Real Life/RL: Our everyday physical world/life.

Region: See SIM.

Resident: Registered virtual world user.

Rez/Rezz: To create an object in-world; also the sharpening of the image seen on the computer monitor screen.

ROI: Abbreviation for "Return on Investment" and refers to the percentage of profit or revenue generated from a specific activity.

RP: Acronym for role play.

RPG: Acronym for role-playing game.

RSS Feed: Acronym for "Real Simple Syndication" which is a format for syndicating news or other content.

Scene: A set of VRML or other 3D format objects that provide a coherent whole, such as a room, building or forest.

Screen Shot/Screen Capture: The act of taking a digital capture of what is on the screen or shown in the current window.

Shared Worlds: Virtual environments with multiple active users.

SIM: An area hosted by a single server. Also called a **region**.

SL: Abbreviation for Second Life.

SLT: Acronym for Second Life Time which is the same as Pacific Standard Time (used because Linden Labs is based in California).

SLURL: Acronym for Second Life URL, a web address for a place on the virtual world Second Life.

Social Media: Tools and platforms to publish, converse and share content online including blogs, wikis, podcasts, and the sites focused on sharing information, stories, photos, audio and video files, and bookmarks.

Social Media Marketing: The planned, usually paid, use of social media to create awareness of a brand, product or specific promotion.

Social Networking: The act of engaging on a social networking site(s).

Social Networking Site: 2D websites where users can post information about themselves, communicate with and interact with other users, share/imbed streaming media, etc. Examples are MySpace and Facebook.

Target Audience: A specified group of ideal customers or potential customers defined by demographics and/or psychographics.

Teleport, Teleporting, TP: Instantaneous transport from one set of coordinates to another moving an avatar from one location to another.

Teleport/Teleporting: The act of transporting an avatar from one location to another within a world.

Terms of Service: The listed guidelines for user behavior as well as any and all legal stipulations. Also known as **Community Standards**.

Text Chat: Communication between two or more avatars by typing on the computer keyboard. Conversations are viewed on the computer screen.

Texture: An image applied to the surface of an object.

Tween: Boy or girl aged 8 to 12 years.

URL: Acronym for Uniform Resource Locator, the address of a page on the Internet.

User Generated Content/UGC: Online content, including text, graphics, video and audio, found on websites and blogs created by individuals rather than traditional media such as commercial broadcasters and production companies.

VW: Abbreviation for "virtual world."

Vehicle/Virtual Vehicle: A scripted object whose movement can be controlled by the user as a form of transportation. Vehicles can be cars, airplanes, hoverboards, boats, UFOs, etc.

Viewpoint: See **Camera Position**.

Viral Marketing: A form of advertising that propagates itself by one person telling another person. Also known as **Word-of-Mouth Marketing**.

Virtual Community: Group congregations and communications online either through the regular Internet or within a virtual world.

Virtual Life/VL: Our life within virtual worlds.

Virtual pet: A 2D or 3D graphic representation of an animal or creature that acts and can be interacted with as one would a real world animal such as by feeding, clothing, walking, etc.

Virtual Reality: Computer-created artificial world in which the user has the impression of being in and interacting with objects in that world.

VLOG/VBLOG: Abbreviation for Video Log/Video Blog.

Voice Chat: Communication between two or more avatars by speaking into a microphone. Voice chat uses Voice Over Internet Protocol (VOIP) technology.

V-pet: Same as virtual pet.

VRML: Virtual Reality Modeling Language, an animated 3D virtual environment specification.

Web 2.0: Term for the current second-generation of Internet services including social networking sites, wikis, virtual worlds, etc.

Web 3.0: Term sometimes used to describe the emerging 3D Internet and related technologies such as 3D virtual worlds.

Wiki: A collaborative website that allows anyone who has access to it to create, add and edit content and information. Example is Wikipedia.

ABOUT THE AUTHOR

Alycia de Mesa is a brand consultant, author, writer and speaker. Alycia's client list includes McDonald's, Frito-Lay, Procter & Gamble, Xerox, HP, Phoenix Coyotes NHL team, WVU and many, many others from start-ups to Fortune 100 across industries from food to sports and entertainment. Over the last two years, she has been a guest speaker at Stanford University's Graduate School of Business "Future of Entertainment" conference and Luxe's Luxury Branding on the Internet conference in Paris, France.

Her published works on branding news, trends, analysis and commentary have appeared around the world most notably for Brandchannel.com and Businessweek.com's Design and Innovation sections. Her book *Before The Brand* was published by McGraw-Hill in 2002 for business audiences.

Alycia graduated from Arizona State University in 1992 with a Bachelor of Arts degree in political science and minor in French language and literature. In addition to consulting and writing, Alycia is a concert grand harpist and composer who gets her kicks bending genres and playing with symphonies to rock bands. She is wife to Bruce and mom to Kian and Kai.

More information on Alycia's brand consultancy can be found at http://www.demesabrands.com and her blog read at http://alyciademesa.blogspot.com

Books and Articles by Alycia de Mesa

Before the Brand: Creating the Unique DNA of Brand Identity, McGraw-Hill (published under the name Alycia Perry)

A complete list of published brand articles by Alycia de mesa can be found at Brandchannel.com http://www. brandchannel.com

INDEX